TOO MANY
MIRACLES

Too Many Miracles
Robin Bee Owens
ISBN-10: 0692627456
ISBN-13:978-0692627457

Published by Inknbeans Press, 2016

Cover art and Picture by: Robin Bee Owens
Interior design by j-views (info@j-views.biz)

www.inknbeans.com
Inknbeans Press, 25060 Hancock Avenue Bldg 103 Suite 458, Murrieta CA 92562, USA

Contents

Acknowledgements

I have so many people to thank, but I will narrow it down to a few.

I want to begin with my publisher for suggesting that I write this book. Writer's block is a tough one to break through and with her encouragement and suggestion, I was able to. Thank you for everything you do for all of us Beans, Jo.

Secondly I want to thank Hugh for editing this book. His expertise, insights, and suggestions were very helpful. Thank you.

Next I want to thank my husband for all of his support. John, you encourage me and support me no matter what hare-brained idea I come up with. Thank you and I love you.

To my parents, thank you for being my parents and teaching me that the only one to stand in my way in anything I desire to do is me. Thank you, Mom and Dad.

My children and grandchildren, I want to thank you for just being wonderful and my biggest fans.

To the people that sent me their testimonies, thank you. God bless you all.

ೋೋ

I took the picture on the cover while visiting this waterfall on the island of Hawaii. Even a waterfall is a miracle. Not only because of the way that God has made them, but also their ability to help people relax when near them.

ೋೋ

TOO MANY MIRACLES

ROBIN BEE OWENS

INKNBEANS PRESS, MURRIETA, CA,
USA

Part I
My Experiences

Too Many Miracles

Too many miracles? How can there be too many miracles? There is no such thing as "too many miracles." There are too many miracles for anyone to convince me that there is no God.

This book gives testimony about the miracles I have personally witnessed or experienced, as well as the testimonies of others.

Some events are explained by science. Technology has improved over the years to help get closer to truths on some things. However, over the years, many of what are now known as theories have been taken as truth. Even our science and history textbooks have changed in their information over the years.

I want to share testimonies on miracles that cannot be explained by science. Even if they can be explained that way, we know Who is really responsible for these miracles. Miracles that are awe-inspiring. Miracles that would be unbelievable – except for the fact that they were first-hand experiences.

I do hope you enjoy these stories as much as I enjoyed writing them.

Chapter 1
In the Beginning...

"In the beginning God created the heavens and the earth." **Genesis 1:1**

I have been raised in church and on the Word of God my whole entire life. My own grandfather was a pastor, so I was brought up to be in church each and every time the doors were open.

At the age of five, I attended my grandfather's church. When he would ask someone to come forward to pray for a member of the church who was very ill, I would go forward. There was a little girl in our church who seemed to be sick quite often. I did not understand why she was sick and missed so much church, but she had an immune deficiency problem. I would go to the altar to stand as a proxy for her and receive prayers each time she was sick and in the hospital. My grandfather and the elders of the church would gather around me, and my grandfather would anoint my forehead with oil in the sign of a cross. After the anointing, my grandfather and the elders would lay hands on me and pray for this little girl.

One Sunday morning, we received news that this little girl was ill once more; she was in the hospital and very sick. The prognosis did not look at all good for her, and the doctors did not believe she would make it out of the hospital alive.

My grandfather told the congregation about this little girl and asked for someone to come forward to stand in her place for prayer. Of course, being only five years old, I was not paying attention to what was being said. My grandmother shoved me out of the pew and had me go forward. Quite comical if you really think about it, a grandmother pushing their granddaughter out of her seat. I went forward, not really knowing why, but I believed

3

God was going to heal someone.

I knelt down at the altar and my grandfather put the oil in the form of a cross on my forehead, the elders placed their hands on my shoulder and my back, my grandfather placed his hands on the top of my head, and the prayer began. Each time my grandfather would say "In the name of Jesus" he pressed down on my head making me bob. This is why I loved going to the altar; I loved the bobbing of my head to go with the words, "In the name of Jesus." Even if I did not fully understand what was happening, God was still using me as a stand-in. In His eyes, I was not there for myself, I was there for this little girl. After the prayer, I went back to my seat and the sermon began.

After we had returned home and changed out of our church clothes, the phone rang, and my mother answered it. I heard her talking to someone and she was a bit excited, but the only thing on my mind was lunch and then a nap (we always took naps after lunch on Sundays.) After grace had been said, over lunch, my mother told me that the little girl was all better and the doctors were surprised. That was the fastest answer to a prayer I had ever witnessed in my young life.

This was the first miracle that I personally experienced.

God made us with His own hands. He spoke everything else into existence, but He scooped up clay from the earth and He made man out of His own image.

"And God said, Let us make man in our image, after our likeness: and let them have dominion over the fish of the sea, and over the fowl of the air, and over the cattle, and over all the earth, and over every creeping thing that creepeth upon the earth." **Genesis 1:26**

God made us and He knows our bodies better than anyone in the world. Because He knows our bodies and He made us, He can fix whatever is wrong with no effort at all. In fact, all He would need to do is speak the words and it is done.

I was an adult before I was hit by the magnitude of how big our God truly is. I was cleaning house when I had to pick up a dust ball. I looked at it in the palm of my hand and it reminded me of the song, "He's got the Whole World in His Hand." Looking at that dust ball and the size of it as it sat in my hand, I thought of that song, I was just dumbfounded at the realization of how mankind appears to God. Man is just a speck. Let me put that another way. We are a speck in comparison to God. Now get this, He came down to earth, scooped up some dirt and formed man. He could have said, "Let there be man and woman," but He didn't. He formed us with His own hands and He breathed His own breath into us. We truly matter to Him. Then He put man to sleep, took his rib, and created woman. Why? Because He even said that it was not good for man to be alone.

Think of a sculptor making a sculpture of man. He would form the clay and press on it and use tools to get the details that he wants. When it is done and it is exactly the way he wanted it, he will then show it off to others. He loves his sculpture.

Let's get to more miracles that I have experienced, shall we?

ᔇᔒ

Chapter 2
My First Personal Miracle...

"That if thou shalt confess with thy mouth the Lord Jesus, and shalt believe in thine heart that God hath raised him from the dead, thou shalt be saved." **Romans 10:9**

A s I wrote in the first chapter, I was raised in church and I have heard all of the Bible stories from the time I was old enough for Sunday school, and even before that, but that doesn't get me a ticket into heaven.

At six years old, sitting in Vacation Bible School in Ocean Springs, Mississippi, I was listening to the teacher telling Bible stories about Jesus' birth, death, and resurrection, and it became clear to me that just because my grandfather was a preacher did not mean that I would go to Heaven. Just because my mom and my dad were saved and going to Heaven did not ensure me of my spot there. I had to accept Christ as my Savior personally. I had to ask Him to forgive me. I had to believe that He came to earth and was born from a virgin. I had to believe that He took my sins and all of the sins of the world to the Cross and He died on that Cross. I had to believe that just three days later, He arose from the dead and defeated death. I had to ask Him to come into my heart and to save me. Save me? Save me from what? you may ask. Save me from Hell's fire and brimstone. Save me from that second death that is eternal and never-ending. In Vacation Bible School in 1967 at the tender age of six, I got on my knees and prayed. I accepted Christ as my personal Lord and Savior.

This is the first personal miracle for me. It doesn't happen to all children at the same age. God knows when the child is ready and will stir their spirit. He will call on them and they will respond.

"Behold, I stand at the door, and knock: if any man hear my voice, and open the door, I will come in to him, and will sup with him, and he with me." **Revelation 3:20**

Any time a person surrenders his life to God, it is a miracle. Think about it this way. How many people turned their backs on Jesus while He walked on this earth? He was here in the flesh, walking among men and they did not accept Him.

We wouldn't be any different. If Jesus were here in His physical form, right now, would you accept Him? We have more faith than the men and women during the time He was here. We accept Him and believe without seeing Him physically.

Not long after I was saved in Vacation Bible School in 1967, I was baptized. The Baptists (of which I am a member) believe in immersion baptism because it represents what happened inside us when we accepted Christ; the old man passes, and behold! A new man is born. We also believe it symbolizes Jesus' death in that when he was taken down from the cross, he was buried and three days later he rose up from the dead.

My mother teased me by saying that my toes were not baptized. You see, I was only seven years old, not long after my birthday, when I was baptized. When the pastor dunked me under the water, my feet floated to the top, and my toes stuck out of the water. It gives us something to laugh about when we talk about those days.

ഐ

Chapter 3
Angels Among Us...

"For he shall give his angels charge over thee, to keep thee in all thy ways." **Psalms 91:11**

I was taught that when we are born, God assigns a guardian angel to us. No, I do not believe that loved ones who have gone on before us become those guardian angels. We were made and placed a little higher than angels, so dying and becoming angels is not the way God has designed things.

As I wrote just now, I was taught that God assigns us a guardian angel when we are born. When I was older, my mother told me of the number of times as a baby when I would watch something up on the ceiling and would smile and gurgle at whatever it was I was seeing. She truly believed it was my guardian angel.

When we reach the age of accountability, our angel returns to Heaven until we accept the Lord, and then our angel comes back to us. This is something I truly believe. No-one has told me of this, nor have I read this in the Bible, it is just something that I feel is true. My own angel came back to me when I accepted the Lord at Vacation Bible School.

I am terrified of the dark. I have always been terrified of the dark. I don't understand why this is so, but that is just the way it is with me. When I was eight years old, I woke up during a black-out in our trailer park. All of the lights, including the street lights, went out. There were no cars on the road because it was around three in the morning. I was scared. Normally, when I was afraid as a child, I would scream bloody murder. My mother often would have the hair on her arms stand on end because of my screams. But on this particular night, I did not scream. I saw a light start to glow in the corner of my room. This light grew until my whole room was flooded with this light, which I could not look at because it was so bright. With my eyes closed, I heard a voice say to me, "Do not be afraid, I am here with you." I felt so comforted that I went right back to sleep. When I told my mom that my guardian angel had spoken to me and what he had said, she asked me how I knew it was a "he" that had spoken to me. I told her that it was a man's voice I heard. This makes sense, because all the angels named in the Bible have masculine names: Gabriel, Michael. My mom told me this.

Whenever I felt afraid after that night, I would remember my angel and thank my Father for sending him to me.

Many, many years later, I heard that voice again, and I will tell you about it later on.

Chapter 4
During the Storm...

"But as they sailed he fell asleep: and there came down a storm of wind on the lake; and they were filled with water, and were in jeopardy. And they came to him, and awoke him, saying, Master, master, we perish. Then he arose, and rebuked the wind and the raging of the water: and they ceased, and there was a calm. And he said unto them, where is your faith? And they being afraid wondered, saying one to another, what manner of man is this! For He commandeth even the winds and water, and they obey him." **Luke 8:23-25**

In 1969, we lived in Biloxi, Mississippi, and our home was a trailer (we call them "mobile homes" today). I wasn't quite nine, that was to be in a few more months. That spring, my parents got a bunny rabbit for my sister and my brother and me. I named him Twinkles because his nose always twitched, and I loved Twinkles.

In August, on our way to church, my brother, sister and I were in the back seat. We were probably arguing and telling each other to stay on their own side of the car like typical young siblings. We were listening to some talk show on the radio, or at least, that is what I thought it was. It turned out to be the news. We were on the way to church, but dad turned the car around and we headed back towards home. When we got home, my parents grabbed a few items, put the rabbit and his cage into the trailer and we left for Keesler Air Force Base. We had to go to Wolf Hall for shelter. I didn't know what was going on. All I knew was that it was strange that we weren't going to church.

"There is a storm coming," was all we were told by our parents.

This storm turned out to be the most devastating storm in Mississippi history until Hurricane Katrina. Hurricane Camille slammed into Mississippi as a category five storm. The winds were sustained at a minimum of 190 mph, with gusts much higher. The one good thing was that the storm hit at low tide. If it had been high tide, then Camille would still hold the record for the worst recorded storm.

We stayed in the crowded, noisy shelter all night. Then the lights went out. Mom called us over to her. She had made a pallet of blankets on the floor under the table for us to sleep on (she slept on top of the table.) My father had to go out into the storm to rescue those who had waited until the last minute to head for shelter. (This is my recollection – remember I was only eight years old, and I'm really not sure now why my dad had to be out in the storm, rescuing others.) We seemed to be in that shelter for ever, only seeing my dad from time to time.

We could hear the winds whipping and whistling around the building. It was scary being there with the lights out, and listening to things being thrown around, and the wind whipping around the building. I was afraid, lying there under the table, next to my brother and sister. The only comfort I had was that my mother was on top of the table, much like the story of a hen sitting on her chicks during a fire to protect them. What I did not understand or realize at the time was that my mother was that mother hen, and that, if the ceiling had caved in, my mother would not be with us today.

After the storm was over and we were given clearance to leave, we headed outdoors to the brightest sunshine ever. Looking around the parking lot, I noticed all the flipped-over cars, those that had run into other cars, or had been flooded. Wow, they looked like the model cars that we would play with under the oak tree at my grandmother's in Virginia. We got to our car – and there wasn't a scratch on the vehicle. It looked as if a glass dome had been placed over our car and protected it from being hit by debris or even by the other cars. My mom thanked God and we got in and headed home.

It usually took us fifteen minutes at the most to go from our house to Keesler Air Force Base, but on this day it took about three hours. The bridges had been washed away and we had to go up north to come back down on our way home. The devastation I saw that day is something I will never forget.

I remember seeing high-rise buildings that had been on the water and were now concrete slabs. There was a shrimp boat in the top of a huge oak tree. On top of the high-rise bridge was a grand piano. Houses were gone, streets were flooded, trees were down, there were cars upside-down or across the lot. Then we arrived home. The trailers around us had been pretty badly damaged. Some were missing windows, some were destroyed due to the water, and some had trees lying across them. Our trailer had little to no damage. A few planks of the metal awning that covered the front had moved over, and there was a small tree limb (actually, more like a large stick) on top of it. No water damage and no glass broken. Even Twinkles was fine, and still in his cage. It looked as though a dome had been placed over our trailer, just like it had over our car in the parking lot during the storm. No scratches on the car, nothing damaged on the trailer. It was amazing.

My mom told me later on that she had said a prayer as daddy was taking us to the shelter. She reminded God that everything we had was because He had allowed us to have it. She said that He could take it all if He wanted, but asked Him to leave us the car, so that we could leave town if need be. God answered her prayers. He left us the car and our home. In all the neighborhood, we had the only running water too. Of course, we were told that we should not drink it because the water was contaminated, but even so, we had running water.

We had to buy water from the water truck and we went to the high school because everyone needed a tetanus shot. Because the water had got under it, the floor of the gymnasium looked like the currents in the Gulf Stream.

My mother ended up having heatstroke and we had to pack up and head to Virginia where we stayed with my grandmother and grandfather until power was restored to our area of Mississippi. The start of school was delayed, but we made up for that by having to go to school on Saturdays for a few weeks.

I have to say our escape from Camille is one of the biggest miracles that I had witnessed at this point in my life.

Chapter 5
Others Among Us...

*"My God hath sent his angel, and hath shut the lions'
mouths, that they have not hurt me: forasmuch as
before him innocency was found in me; and also before
thee, O king, have I done no hurt."* **Daniel 6:22**

I have written about seeing my angel as a baby, and then again at the age of eight. It seems the gift God has given my mother's side of the family is the ability to sense spirits – and I am not talking about the ghosts you hear about on TV. To be honest, despite everything that has happened in my life that I cannot understand, I only believe in two kinds of spirits: angels and demons. I have seen both.

My grandmother lived in a house in Newport News, Virginia, that was very active. Most people would claim they were ghosts, but I know from the feelings I got from them that they were not ghosts. These were not good spirits at all.

This house was really creepy upstairs, and also in the basement. Every afternoon, at four o'clock, you would hear someone come in through the front door and walk up the stairs into one of the bedrooms. The bedroom door would close and that was it. If you went up there, you would find all of the doors open and no one upstairs. I believe houses can record what some people might call "residual spirits." The place remembers an event that took place over and over again, every day of every year. In essence, the floor and the steps remember the creaks, and they just creak away, the same hour every day. Anyway, that is my theory.

Other things which were not good would happen in that house. My sister and I shared a second floor room to the left of the stairs. There was a closet in our room, and another door to another staircase, leading to the attic. Every night, the handle to the attic door would jiggle, and this scared both my sister and me. My sister would even put popsicle sticks all around the handle in the evening, but the next morning, the sticks would be lying on the floor with the door open about an inch.

One morning, I had to go upstairs to brush my teeth for school. My dad was on an unaccompanied tour (which means the military had him move to a location without us), so we moved in with my grandparents. While I was alone upstairs, I heard someone laugh. It was an evil laugh, sounding much like a laugh of a wicked witch that you might hear in a "princess" movie. The hair on my arms stood up and chills went down my spine. I ran downstairs – and did not brush my teeth that day. A week later, while I was again alone upstairs, I heard a loud growl.

Don't get me wrong. The house was not "haunted" by the spirits of dead people, as some in the paranormal field would want you to think. It was filled with evil spirits. There were invisible birds diving down toward your head, dark shadows, and curtains billowing out when the windows were covered in plastic.

After I was grown and had children of my own, my grandmother told me that she would like to move back into that house and buy it, as they had only been renting it before. I told her that if she did, I would visit her but my children would not set foot in that house.

A year or two after I heard those sounds I just mentioned, and after living in that house with my grandparents, we moved to Fort Lee, Virginia. I was then fourteen and we were living on base.

I was in my rebellious years. My parents no longer went to church, and they did not make us go to church either. I still believed in Jesus and I still prayed to Him, but I was also rebellious. I didn't do anything seriously wrong, but if I had kept on the track I was going, there was no telling how I might have ended up. The worst thing I did at this time was starting to smoke cigarettes. Most of my friends were doing pot and drinking alcohol, but I, and a few of my friends, only smoked cigarettes. It made us feel so big. Pretty dumb when you think about it. When I wasn't home, I was walking around post, smoking with my friends, laughing, cutting up, starting to curse from time to time, and getting into fights. I felt bad about the cursing and the fighting. What I mean here is that my conscience got to me. I don't understand why I started doing these things, but looking back, it was hardly a time in my life of which I am proud.

One night, I was thinking about some bad things, and I was angry with my sister and my parents about something. You know, thinking back on them today, I have no clue what it was all about. While I was lying reading a book on my bed, I heard laughter. This was evil laughter, much like the laughter I heard when I was twelve, but not so witch-like. I looked up, and there on my bedroom door was a face looking at me, laughing. It was Satan. Of course he can take any form he wants, but he wanted me to know it was him, so he took the form in which we normally think of him, with a red face, horns, pointed chin, and evil eyes. I was terrified, and I started praying.

Many nights after that, I would hear something in our room that would wake me up from a deep sleep, but I was too terrified to move. I felt that if I moved, "it" would get me. Unknown to me, until much later, my sister heard the same thing, and felt the same way about it. We would lie very still and would barely breathe until the sun came up. We would talk about the event and realized that we both were waiting for the other to move first. I went back to reading my Bible and I quit using bad language, I even stopped hanging out with the girls who had been leading me down the wrong path. We would hold séances and we played with an ouija board, against everything what I was taught. I had been taking it as all being in fun, but doorways were being opened, and I believe God allowed me to see the enemy to straighten me out. It worked. After that, I no longer did séances or even allowed an ouija board into my house. I still have friends and acquaintances who will worship everything and anything other than God. I don't understand how they cannot see that God is real and that He loves them. He loves all of us.

"For God so loved the world that he gave his only begotten Son, that whosoever believeth in him should not perish, but have everlasting life." **John 3:16**

I know He loves me. I know, you are asking how this is a miracle. It is a miracle because I straightened up. I was heading down the wrong path and God allowed things to happen to straighten me up. If He had not allowed me to experience these things, no telling what else I would have got into, quite apart from smoking cigarettes.

ৎৄৎ

Chapter 6
Physical Healings...

"And great multitudes came unto him, having with them those that were lame, blind, dumb, maimed, and many others, and cast them down at Jesus' feet; and he healed them:" **Matthew 15:30**

Y ou heard about my first witness of healing, with the little girl in my church. Even though I was really young, it did make an impression.

This is a miracle that was told to me by my mother and grandmother. My mother told me that when she was a child, she ended up having to take care of her family because my grandmother was diagnosed with cancer (I believe it was either uterine or cervical) – usually a death sentence in those days, but she went to the hospital for surgery to remove the cancer.

This part of the miracle was told to me by my grandmother. On the night prior to the operation, a bright light came into her room, moved over her, and she felt warmth in her mid-section. The light hovered there for a moment and then went away. She lay there in her hospital bed, wondering what had just happened.

The doctors carried out more tests and X-rays before surgery, and were stunned to see that there was no longer any cancer. In fact, it appeared as though she had scar tissue, as if she had already undergone surgery.

My grandmother lived for many years after that, dying when she was in her 70s, and I was grown with two children of my own.

My grandparents took in foster children, who witnessed and lived through things no child should ever experience. From these children, I learned just how blessed I am to have my parents. I really felt for these kids. One child suffered from severe disabilities: cerebral palsy; her fingers and toes bent and twisted, and her speech was such that she had her own language. She never knew she was hungry and wouldn't eat without being told to, and we would play eating games with her just to get her to eat. At three years old, she looked like a walking skeleton.

My grandparents loved this girl so much they ended up adopting her. She was a challenge, and for a long time I was very jealous of her, because she ended up getting the attention that my cousins, my siblings and I used to receive. As I grew into an adult, I knew it was okay. She did lie about all of us to our grandparents, just to make my grandmother angry with us; but again, now that I am grown up, I have forgiven her. But what was this girl's miracle? Here it is.

Her fingers and toes were badly bent and twisted, and there wasn't a straight finger on her. Her toes were so bad that she literally walked on the tips of her feet, like a ballerina. The doctors discussed carrying out surgery to straighten out her fingers and toes, but my grandparents laid hands on her and prayed. I believe she was around seven years old at the time. The very next day after they had prayed, they took her to the doctors for them to see. Her feet had completely straightened and she only had one bent finger. This girl will tell everyone that will listen that all of her hands and her toes once looked like that one bent finger. She will tell everyone that "Jesus healed me." She is now able to talk properly and everyone can understand her. Did you notice that? She tells people that Jesus healed her.

When she was about twelve, about the age when she should start her monthly menstrual cycle, my grandparents took her to the doctor to be examined. My grandmother knew something was not right, because she was showing signs of developing but was not having her cycle. The doctors said, after they had examined her, that they needed to do surgery to create a vaginal opening. They added that if they did not create an opening and she started her periods, there was no exit, the discharge would end up crystalizing, and the result could be fatal. Either she had been born without this opening, or it had closed up when she was an infant. Since she had been in foster care from birth, they could not say for sure which it was. She was to come in with my grandparents the next morning to prep for surgery. When they got home, my grandparents laid hands on her once again and prayed over her. When they took her for her pre-operation prepping, the doctors were amazed. She not only had a vaginal opening, she had started her monthly cycle. The doctors told my grandparents that there was no explanation except for God. They truly believed God had healed her.

$$\wp\gamma\wp$$

Chapter 7
Healed

"And his fame went throughout all Syria: and they brought unto him all sick people that were taken with divers diseases and torments, and those which were possessed with devils, and those which were lunatick, and those that had the palsy; and he healed them." **Matthew 4:24**

A s an adult, I started going to an Assembly of God Church and learning about a loving God. The church I grew up in (not my grandfather's) taught of a vengeful God. Of course, yes, the Bible does say that God tells us that vengeance is His. I had felt that God was there watching every move I was making, just waiting for me to trip up, so He can punish me. This new church was teaching me of a loving God who would admonish me when I messed up but who still loved me and would help me learn from all of my mistakes. I was learning so much from this church, and realized that this is where God wanted me to be at that moment.

The church was holding a tent revival in a very poor section of our community, a section of town that you really wouldn't want to be in, especially at night. We would all go together on a bus and would sit in the tent, welcoming all the neighbors who came over to see what was going on. Of course there were those who claimed to be Satanists, trying to destroy the ministry, but our God is so much stronger than their beliefs.

One evening, during the service, I noticed a young boy who was obviously deaf, as when I welcomed them to the meeting, he could talk, but with the obvious speech pattern of deaf people. This is so different that it cannot be duplicated perfectly by a hearing person, much less by a young boy. I know this because my last church had started a deaf ministry where I met several deaf people and there is a person in my family who is deaf, and their speech pattern is unique.

The pastor asked if there was anyone in the meeting who knew sign language, but there was no-one. I hadn't used it in so long, there was no way I could interpret what the pastor was saying. We all prayed for God to help this child learn from the lesson.

The boy's grandfather was sitting next to him, trying his best to interpret what the pastor was saying. The grandfather knew very little sign language, but he was trying hard. However, I noticed that the boy kept signing to his grandfather that he could hear the pastor. The grandfather was skeptical and kept signing what the pastor was saying as best he could, and the boy kept signing that he could hear the pastor.

At the end of the service we hold what we call the "invitational hymn and altar call," where people are invited to come forward if they want to learn more about Jesus, want to accept Jesus or want to pray at the altar. This boy and his grandfather came forward. The pastor was ecstatic and proclaimed to the rest of us that the boy was claiming to hear him. The pastor would demonstrate this by having the boy turn his back to him and to look at the congregation. The pastor would say something and the boy's eyes really widened before he slowly turned around to look at the pastor. The pastor would repeat his question to him "Son, do you hear me?" The boy nodded his head. Yes. He was able to read lips, so he understood the question when it was asked the second time after he had turned around, but while his back was to the pastor, he could hear the sound of the words, though he had no clue what the pastor was saying, because he had never heard speech before.

That same night, his grandfather accepted Christ as his Lord and Savior. This made it a double miracle. Most seniors are set in their ways, and it is very hard to lead them to Christ. It is possible, but very difficult because they believe what they have always believed, and no one can tell them differently. The Lord used the healing of his grandson's hearing to prove to this old man that He really does exist, and that He does care for the least of them.

Now for a personal healing. In the late nineties, my husband received orders from the military to move to Baltimore, Maryland. We attended a Church of God off and on but for a couple of years we did not find a church to attend regularly. In 2001, Lighthouse Baptist Church started, with the first service being held on April 1 (April Fool's Day) and this was more like the churches I grew up in. I felt that this was the perfect opportunity to give my family an idea of how I grew up.

Since we moved to Maryland, every October I developed an allergy problem, where I would end up with bronchitis and ultimately lose my voice until March or April. This is hard for me, especially around Christmas, since I love singing Christmas carols. I didn't even have a squeak. Total silence. I would see the doctor, and he put it down to inflammation of my vocal cords, due to allergies and bronchitis, and there was nothing he could do about it. My throat wasn't sore, it was just that I had no voice. Of course, my family may have enjoyed the peace and quiet because I had no voice. But as far as that went, along with the good always comes the bad. I would always have my voice back by Easter, and since I couldn't sing Christmas carols at Christmas, I would sing all of them during Easter. I had the last laugh with that one.

October 2001 was no different for me. I would start off with congestion, then I would start coughing uncontrollably, and then the voice would go. There was one young man in our church who was physically and mentally challenged, and he started making fun of me because I could not talk. Not a vicious type of mocking, you understand, just all in fun. He kept me laughing every Sunday and Wednesday night. He would come up to me and ask, "Can you talk?" I would shake my head and mouth the word "no." He would just start laughing, because he found it all very amusing. I loved that young man. He had the sort of life and innocence in him that I only see in very young children, or in people with challenges like his.

When this started up again in 2002, I felt enough was enough. While I still had a little bit of voice left in me, I went to the pastor and asked him if he believed in anointing with oil and prayer. He said that since it was all biblical, that he indeed did believe. I asked to be prayed over for the loss of my voice. My husband, the pastor, and one other member met with me in the pastor's office. The pastor took a vial of oil from his desk drawer and he read from the Bible. He said to us that what he was going to do would only work if the one asking to have this done truly believes. I truly believed this would work. I feel it is taking the step of faith a bit further and pushing right through to the throne of God. I was anointed and prayed over. By the end of the week, my voice was better. I never fully lost my voice that year; and since that time, I have never lost my voice. I might get hoarse, but I have not lost my voice completely since that time.

Now for the best physical healing I have ever witnessed, with my dad being the recipient of this miracle.

I have acid reflux and I also have Barrett's Disease with the need to have an endoscopy done every two years. I finally convinced my dad that he needed to have one done because he has had acid indigestion for as long as I can remember. He reluctantly decided to talk to his doctor about this.

Barrett's Disease, by the way, is a condition where acid has corroded the esophagus over a long period of time, changing the cells within to be like those found in the intestines. The esophagus is not the place for this sort of cell to be. My Barrett's is known as short segment Barrett's, which needs to be checked on a regular basis and I need medication to slow the production of acid in my stomach. Long segment Barrett's is more serious, and if you have this form, you need an endoscopy every six months, or a year at most. The next stage after Barrett's is dysplasia, followed by esophageal cancer.

My dad was diagnosed with long segment Barrett's (it seems I inherited the tendency from him). I knew the doctor told both my parents how severe this form was, but reassured them that it was still manageable. A year went by and the doctor never called my dad to schedule an appointment. Because this is something that their doctors would normally do, my dad called him, and another endoscopy was scheduled. This time my dad was diagnosed with high dysplasia, and the doctor felt that surgery to remove his esophagus and attach his stomach up to his throat would be the best option for him. The doctor was sure the recovery time would be minimal, and my dad would be home in no time at all. This was a different treatment to that which my cousin received. There, the spots were removed, and he had radiation treatment. His esophagus and throat eventually became hard as concrete and he passed away.

The surgery proceeded and my dad was placed in ICU afterwards for observation, but something went wrong. He woke up, grabbed his tube in his throat, and shoved it down his throat before yanking it out, puncturing a hole in his intestines. Bile ended up in his bloodstream and in his lungs. He ended up staying in ICU for seven weeks, and the doctors were not convinced that he would survive.

My family started praying. I took my dad and his situation to my church to be on the prayer list. My mom had everyone in her church praying. Their pastor would visit and pray for him. The waiting room was always filled with members of their Sunday school class. There was constant prayer for my dad, and saying that does not even touch on the amount of prayer going to the Throne. We had people all over the country, if not all over the world, praying for him.

After about seven weeks of going back and forth between Pasadena, Maryland and Chesapeake, Virginia, I finally told my mom that she needed to have my dad anointed and prayed over. She asked me to make the request to my church to do this, but

I reminded her that she was married to him, which meant they were one in God's eyes. She had to be the one making the request, since her husband, my father, was not in a condition to do so. She talked to her pastor and he agreed.

Once the pastor and the elders had anointed my dad's head and prayed over him, the healing process accelerated. My dad was soon out of ICU and in his own room. A couple of days after that, he was sent home. I teasingly tell my mom, "I told you so", but I only pick on her about this because I know she knew this would work. However, she was just too close to the situation to think of doing this. She would go home and pray, even lying on the floor, face down, praying when no one was around.

When dad, went to the doctor for his first follow-up examination, the doctor called him by his first name and then added "Lazarus" (his real middle name is Randall) because he didn't think my dad had been going to live, and he had truly felt my dad had been right at death's door.

ゆ

Chapter 8
The Power of Prayer

"And all things, whatsoever ye shall ask in prayer, believing, ye shall receive." **Matthew 21:22**

Jesus tells that whatever we will ask in prayer, believing, we will receive an answer. The key word is 'believing.'

I have met so many people in my life. With my dad being military and my husband being military, my life has been one of always moving. Of the people I have met in my life, there are many that do not believe in prayer or in God. When I asked them why they do not believe, they would answer that none of their prayers ever got answered. When I ask them if they believed while in prayer, some would say 'no' and that they were testing to see if Christians were correct.

First, God cannot hear prayers if you do not accept Him first. We are so covered with sin and God hates sin. He cannot even look at it. When His Son, Jesus, was on the cross, He represented all of the sins of the world. The Father turned His back. That is when everything went dark. Jesus even called up before He took his last breath. He asked God why He has forsaken Him. Then He died.

If all are sinners, then why can God hear only the prayers of a true believer? It is because when we asked Jesus into our lives, we are then covered with His blood. I envision our prayers as going through the blood and having the sin filtered out. It becomes pure when it gets to the throne of God.

Secondly, all prayers are answered. Some are not answered exactly how we want. Sometimes the answer is a flat out "No." Then there is the answer of "Not right now", and the answer we all want to hear, "Yes." The best way to explain why God answers with all of these is to use the analogy of a parent and a child.

A child goes to their mother to ask if they can build a fire in the backyard. They enjoyed the bonfire dad had back there the night before and wanted to have another one. Of course, the mother being wise in what is good and not good for her child, will tell this child no. The child could be seriously hurt or they could end up having a fire so large that it eventually burns down the house. The mother knew what was best in this scenario.

Another example. A fifteen year old girl is "in love" with a sixteen year old boy. He asks her on a date to go see a movie. She goes and asks her parents if she can go. The parents have never met this boy and knows nothing of who he is, or who his parents are. They would like to get to know the young man before they let their daughter go on a date with him. So the answer the girl gets is "not right now." The parents know that the girl is ready to date, but they want to make sure the girl is with someone that will treat her right.

Another example. A child comes in after playing all morning in the sun. He asks for a glass of water. Knowing that he has played hard and that water is essential for his well-being, of course the answer is yes.

God is our Heavenly Father. He knows what is best for us. He sees the future and knows which answer to give us.

৩৶

Chapter 9
He Provides for Me

"Who provideth for the raven his food? When his young ones cry unto God, they wander for lack of meat." **Job 38:41**

My "Job time" came when I was married to my first husband. For reasons of anonymity, I will call him Jay. Things were great in the very beginning, during dating and the first couple of months after marriage. After that time, things went downhill very quickly. All sorts of abuse went on, mainly verbal, emotional and psychological. To say we were toxic for each other is putting it mildly.

After eleven years of this, I had finally had enough. I asked Jay to leave and he did. During the next six months, I was searching for work, but there was none to be had. Jay did pay for the house and utilities, but only gave me twenty dollars every two weeks to pay for food for our children. He quit paying for the car and used that to cause me anxiety by telling me that it was going to be re-possessed any time.

Our daughters' (we have two) school provided emergency free breakfasts and lunches for them when I asked for it. My mother would watch them after school, and although I ended up going to school to learn a skill, I still could not find a job. My mother would feed my girls with dinner several nights a week.

Until I started school, I would fix dinner for my girls at home and I would exercise while they ate. When I look back, I am still amazed how much food I could get for my children with twenty dollars. I would buy a package of hot dogs, a box of frozen fish sticks, boxed macaroni and cheese (a dollar for four boxes) and canned green beans and pork 'n' beans, cereal and milk. That was all I could buy for two weeks and we would be down to just enough for the girls to eat on that last day before we got twenty dollars again. I did not make the girls clean their plates, and I would eat their scraps. I lost over fifty pounds in three months, the most I have ever lost. It's not a diet plan I would recommend to anyone!

During this time, I would cry, pray and read my Bible. In fact, I would copy the books of Psalms and Proverbs into a notebook each night. With little sleep and two girls to raise, I honestly felt I was hitting the proverbial rock bottom. Looking back, I am still amazed and cannot fathom how I survived this. My daughters never knew the severity and hardship of this time in our lives until they were grown.

When Jay left us, my daughters were afraid, understandable because children feel their daddy is strong and can keep all of the bad things away. This was so with my girls, even if they did see and hear the fights and arguments when we were together.

The night he left, my girls and I were in bed. Everything in the house was very quiet. Out of nowhere, it sounded like someone had gone into my kitchen and they were throwing every dish and plate in the cabinet against the wall and shattering them. My girls came running into my room and climbed into my bed. We cuddled and held each other throughout the night. The sounds of breaking crockery went on until the wee hours of the morning, and then they ended.

The next morning, I went into the kitchen – you can be sure that I was cautious – to see what the mess in there was like. I was totally astounded to find nothing out of place and not a single dish broken. I know what you might think; it must have been a neighbor making the noises in his house, but I can tell you that it was not. We had bought an acre of land and had our house built in a brand new community, and we did not have neighbors at that time. The noise was from inside my house.

Even though I had kept myself pure until marriage, and I had tried hard to make this marriage work, I came to realize that not everyone is raised in the way that I was raised, and may not know how to love. That was the case with my ex-husband, who lacked a role model for what a marriage should be, since his parents divorced when he was a child.

Now, I do not have any animosity towards him. I have forgiven him and I pray for him, asking that no one look at him with anger or ascribes blame. It takes two to make a marriage, and I know I have had faults in this regard as well.

The following is what my youngest experienced during this time.

"I was about six years old and this was about the time you and dad were separated and were going through divorce. The power went out and I was scared. You know how afraid of the dark I am. I started praying like you taught us to pray. I was letting Jesus know I was scared and asked him to hold me. When I finished, I opened my eyes but I couldn't keep my eyes open. There was a really bright light over me, it was hanging right over top of me. I had to close my eyes. I felt a peace come over me and it felt like I was picked up and held. I was comforted and was no longer afraid. I went to sleep."

ᔕᏱᕐ

Chapter 10
Feeling Abandoned

"And Gideon said unto him, Oh my Lord, if the LORD be with us, why then is all this befallen us? and where be all his miracles which our fathers told us of, saying, Did not the LORD bring us up from Egypt? but now the LORD hath forsaken us, and delivered us into the hands of the Midianites." **Judges 6:13**

During the time of my separation leading up to my divorce, I often felt God had abandoned me. I felt that I was not worthy to be loved by anyone. I felt as though I was ugly, fat and a horrible person. I didn't even feel I was a good mom, no matter how many times my daughters would come to me and put their arms around my neck. No matter how many times they would tell me they loved me, I felt very unlovable.

For most of my adult life I was constantly being told that every part of my body was ugly, and that no-one would want to be with me. I was told that I would never make it in this world. I was told to get a job and then told to quit my job. My résumé looked horrible.

After months of throwing a pity party for myself, I got up and brushed myself off. I tried for a job with the Army, but I was a single mom and overweight, and they told me that if I gave up custody of my children, they would take me. I could not do that, as my children had already gone through their dad leaving them and not fighting for custody. They definitely did not need their mom leaving them as well.

I got a job cleaning rooms with a hotel chain, but evidently this was not where God wanted me. After one week of working there, they failed to call me with my schedule. When I called them, I was told that I wasn't on the schedule. I tried again the next week. Again I was told I wasn't on the schedule. I knew then that I did not have a job any more.

What was I going to do? I signed up for school. I started going to a technical school in Virginia Beach, Virginia and started training to be a medical computer specialist (that just means I was training to be a medical receptionist.)

I still had days when I felt isolated from God. I didn't understand why I felt I was in a desert all alone. At night, after the girls were in bed and asleep I prayed and I cried. I would call my family and friends and would talk well into the night. One male friend, who had gone through a similar experience just the year before, would talk to me for hours. We would fall asleep while talking on the phone. One night, after reading my Bible and writing in my journal, I started having anxiety attacks. I called this male friend, only because it was one o'clock in the morning and everyone else I knew was in bed and had to be at work the next day.

This friend was also in bed, and he had to be at work in the morning, but we talked and I cried. Finally, he told me he was coming over to see me. An hour later, he was with me. He got into my bed, fully clothed, lay there, and just held me while I slept. Nothing happened and he behaved as a complete gentleman. He just knew I needed to be held, and that night, I fell in love with this man. Any man who is willing to hold a woman all night, while she looks horrible from crying so much, and not start anything, is a real caring man. He even left early the next morning so that my daughters would not see him. He didn't want them to think bad things about their mother and they had not yet had a chance to meet him.

You may wonder how I came to know this man. We met and dated in high school when he was two years ahead of me, but even after all those years, we remained very good friends. In fact, we got along better as friends than we did when we were dating. After high school, we would continue to talk by phone every six months or so, just enough to continue our friendship and to help each other with the important decisions in our lives, but not enough to prevent any problems with our spouses. We let our spouses know when we talked to each other. In fact one conversation I had was mostly with his spouse. I was so happy for him, as he seemed to be in a perfect marriage with a woman whom he called his "singing angel." They had a baby girl, but about a year later, his wife left him. He was devastated.

〰

I was so confused during this period of my life. I was always taught that marriage is forever and that God does not approve of divorce. I couldn't see how God would approve of the way I was being treated and the way my marriage was going. After I made the decision to ask my husband to leave, I felt such relief and peace come over me.

My friend (the one I mentioned just now) came over one day and brought a case of drinks with him. He also brought his daughter, so that she and my girls could play together. When he placed the drinks in my refrigerator, he started opening the freezer and the cabinets in my kitchen. I have twenty-two cabinets in my kitchen and he opened every one of them. Next thing I knew, he told me that he had forgotten something and asked if I could watch his daughter. Of course I told him that I would watch her. He left, and an hour later, he returned with six bags of groceries. Tears formed in my eyes, and he hugged me. He said he didn't know how hard my life was until he looked in my refrigerator and saw a small container of milk, a tub of margarine and a pitcher of water. He looked in the freezer and saw a package of ham hock that had been given to me and a tray of ice. He looked in the cabinets and saw nothing, because it was the day before I got my twenty dollars for food from my ex-husband. My friend went out and bought me chicken, pork, vegetables, mashed potato mix, macaroni and cheese, bread, peanut butter, jelly, and so many other things that I cannot remember them all. All for me and my girls.

Some of you may be thinking, "How is this a miracle?" We did not get our twenty dollars for food the next day. God knew it wasn't coming. I would have had no food for my children. What God did was to use my friend to get me some food. It wasn't much by most people's standards, perhaps, but it was worth a million dollars and more to me.

It wasn't long after this incident that this friend and my mother started talking and then they ganged up on me – suggesting that I should move in with my mother. It wasn't that I had never thought about doing this; it was because I had been told for my entire adult life that I could not manage on my own, and I wanted to prove that I could. They pointed out to me that I really wasn't doing it on my own. I was dying because I was starving. It was situational and not intentional, but I wasn't eating. I was making sure the food I did have would stretch out the two weeks for my daughters, and doing what most moms would do, feeding my children first. I only ate what they left on their plates, and most of the time that was nothing.

My husband left us in March, and I moved in with my mom in September. God kept me alive that whole time without enough food to live on. After moving in with my mother, I no longer felt I was in a desert. I look back and wonder how I survived that time. Then I would remember, smile and thank God for His mercy and His grace. God is good all of the time.

৯৫২

Chapter 11
God Uses Man to Perform Miracles

*"And God wrought special miracles by
the hands of Paul:"* **Acts 19:11**

God uses man all of the time to do many of His miracles. It isn't the man (or woman) who does the miracle, but God through the person. Miracles happen every day through ordinary measures, and by ordinary men and women. The news media sometimes refers to some of these people as "good Samaritans", such as a biker saving a child from a burning building, or another driver pulling a baby out of a car that has been under frigid water for several hours. The world does not look at these as miracles, which is truly sad. They are missing out on God's presence.

〰

God used my male friend to help me out in a difficult time. After living several months with my mom and dad, God allowed me to find a job so that I could move out and live with my brother, who was a policeman in Hampton, Virginia at that time. We got an apartment and we all moved in together, my daughters, my brother and myself in a three-bedroom apartment. I felt I was starting to live again, but my testing was not finished.

Not long after we moved in together, my elder daughter started with an attitude that I did not know how to deal with. I was totally at a loss because I had never experienced this myself. Even while I was growing up, I never experienced what she was going through at that time. She had so much anger and hatred. I thought it was because we moved away from North Carolina and her grandmother, whom she loved so much, and still does to this day. I would discipline her and send her to her room, but things

36

went from bad to worse.

𝍌

She would start to yell at me, screaming obscenities and in be-tween these outbursts, would grab her head and yell that her brain was going to explode. I honestly thought I was living in a scene from "The Exorcist" where the girl turns her head through three hundred sixty degrees and spews pea soup. I started pray-ing over her and pleading the blood (something my grandmother taught me[1]) on her, since I truly thought my daughter was pos-sessed. When that did not help, which it would have if she had truly been possessed, I took her to the doctor, and it turned out that my daughter was suffering episodes of psychomotor sei-zures. That was the beginning of many long days and nights. I spent many nights in the hospital, and in doctors' and psychia-trists' offices. I took her to church and had her prayed over. So much was happening and the trials and errors began.

Seizure after seizure, doctor after doctor but nothing helped. The treatments slowed the seizures down, but then my daughter's

---

1 I want to explain "pleading the blood." as my grandmother taught me. Satan and the demons cannot stand the blood of Jesus. When they are around and a believer sees them or feels their presence, I will say "I bind you in the name of Jesus and I plead the blood of Jesus on you and command you to leave." They have to listen because I believe at that moment, the angels of the Lord are given the extra strength to fight them off. I will also "plead the blood" on my doors and windows once they are gone to prevent them from coming back. It is much like the message of Moses during Passover. He would have all of the Israelites place blood over their doors and door posts as God com-manded them so that death would pass them by. "For the LORD will pass through to smite the Egyptians; and when he seeth the blood upon the lintel, and on the two side posts, the LORD will pass over the door, and will not suffer the destroyer to come in unto your houses to smite you." **Exodus 12:23**
There is power in the blood of Jesus.

weight went out of control, as one side-effect of the medications was weight gain. At eleven years old, she tipped the scale at one hundred twenty five pounds. I asked the doctor for help, but we were referred to a nutritionist who said that she was fine, but to make sure she doesn't gain any more weight. What was that meant to mean? How can you stop an eleven year old who is still growing from putting on weight? We tried and tried to keep her from gaining weight, but we failed. Then the doctor decided to try a new medication for her seizures. It was wonderful! Not only did it control the seizure, it helped her lose weight. But then this medication was pulled off of the shelves, as there were some serious dangers that could not be treated. Of course, with the possibility of those dangers, I was not going to put my daughter's health at any more risk, so we put her back on the medication that had worked before, but with the side-effect of weight gain.

I watched my daughter grow, and the anger continued to grow and build up in her. The end result was that there was nothing more I could do for her. She told me that she wanted to live with her dad. As much as it hurt me, I had to let her go. Life in our home became quite a lot quieter, but I was punishing myself for letting my daughter go to live with her dad. I wanted her with me. She was my first-born, my sweet little girl, but I didn't understand what was going on with her.

※

Living with her dad, she changed even more. When she visited our home, she was respectful and there were almost no outbursts. Visiting us was a different matter to living with us. At her dad's, she was staying out at all hours of the night, with no supervision at all. She had no respect for her stepmother. In the end, her father kicked her out after she graduated from high school. Again, he chose himself over his own children, but I forgive him that. She came back to us, broken and sad. We gave her a place to live and sent her to college. She started going to church with us and she listened to the messages.

🝫

One day, after the morning service, she asked me if she could speak to the pastor after church. I told her yes, that would be okay, but maybe I would be able to help her. She told me she wanted to follow Jesus. I was so elated. I told her that she didn't need the pastor to do this. I sat with her on the top of our staircase and showed her the Bible. I showed her how much Jesus loves her, how He took our sins and had them nailed to the cross with Him. I showed her how He was buried and how He rose from the dead and is now sitting on the right hand side of the throne. I showed her that all she had to do was reach out and accept the gift of life He has for her. She and I sat there and prayed together. She accepted the Lord Jesus as her Savior.

That was the first miracle. She did go to talk to the pastor after the service and told him what had happened and that she wanted to make a public profession and that she wanted to be baptized. I had never been as proud of her as I was at that moment.

🝫

The second miracle was truly for me. Growing up in church, I was surrounded by Christians. I never once saw someone do a complete turnaround in their life. I had never witnessed a change in a person once they became a Christian, but I have seen it with my daughter. I have seen such a complete change in her that you would never believe what she was like before. Unless you had known her in her previous life, you wouldn't know how big a deal this change really is. She studies the Bible every day, looking for truths to share.

Years later, when my daughter became an adult and was with her husband, God showed His hand and another miracle happened. I will tell you about this later on when I write about the miracles other people have experienced.

🝫

Chapter 12
My Guardian Angel

"The angel of the LORD encampeth round about them that fear him, and delivereth them." **Psalm 34:7**

All of the children have now grown, married and two have children of their own. My husband and I are back in Maryland, but living in Glen Burnie – not the ideal place where we would to live, especially after living five years in Hawaii, but this is where the Army has sent us.

I am lying in bed, in a deep sleep with my husband next to me. You know the kind of deep sleep where, you hear nothing and you don't move. In fact, you aren't even dreaming. Next thing I know, I hear my mother say my full name.

When you were younger, maybe your mom called you by your full name when you did something wrong and you instantly knew that you were in trouble. I hear my full name, I sit straight up and say out loud, "Yes ma'am?" I am now awake and looking around the room, and then I realize that my mother did not say my name and I am now an adult. After all, I am now in my fifties.

It seems that one of the gifts of the women in my family is that when one of us thinks hard about another family member, we can hear them subconsciously. For example, if my mother thinks of my name over and over again, I will pick up the phone and call her. She will laugh and say to me, "it still works," and it has become a bit of a joke between us. Sometimes we will call her and ask what she wants.

After hearing her clearly in the middle of that night, the next morning I called her. I asked if she was thinking about me or if she had a dream about me. She told me that she hadn't and asked me why. I told her about her voice waking me up. Her explanation made perfect sense. She told me that maybe I quit breathing in the night and the only voice I would respond to would have been hers. She said that God might have had my guardian angel sound like her to wake me up.

A few weeks later, I was once again deeply asleep, and past the REM stage. I heard a whisper in my ear, and I told myself that I knew that voice! Once before in my life, I heard that voice, back when I was a child, and I woke up in the dark. My guardian angel came close to my ear and whispered my name. I could even feel the breath on my ear. I woke up, sat up and then I prayed and thanked God for waking me up.

ᔦᖾ

Chapter 13
God Shows Miracles as a Witness that He is Still Here

"God also bearing them witness, both with signs and wonders, and with divers miracles, and gifts of the Holy Ghost, according to his own will?" **Hebrews 2:4**

I have given you many miracles I have experienced personally, but now here are a few more things that have happened to those around me, from my point of view, as well as things that have happened to me personally. Here are a few that have happened over the last few years.

While we lived in Pasadena, Maryland, so many miracles happened. First, I want to share the story of the survival of my daughter and son-in-law.

First, I should mention that I have remarried. The man I married was the same friend who helped me during the time I was starving.

My husband is in the military and was away from home on what the military calls TDY (Temporary Duty). I received a phone call letting me know that my oldest daughter had been in a serious car accident. Apparently, she had suffered a seizure while driving, and had hit a house at an incredible speed. The house had been knocked three feet from its foundations, and the car was totally wrecked. The police told my daughter that such an accident would usually kill those involved. My daughter was not treated correctly by the EMTs or the hospital and to this day, she has problems that arise from that accident. Her account of the accident comes later in this book, but this is what I heard.

From what I was told, God took over the wheel of her car,

which was originally heading towards a tree and swerved at the last moment to hit the house. During my daughter's seizure, the car crossed six railroad tracks in a row, which always have trains running along them, but there was no train on the tracks at that time. The car went through S-curves at over 50 miles per hour and stayed on the road. It was meant for her to hit that particular house, which turned out to belong to a pastor and his wife.

This is my daughter's testimony about this incident.

"Another miracle will have to be my car accident. The fact is that I was able to drive down an S-shaped street, missing a huge tree and crashing into a home just a couple of minutes after the children had left the area that I drove my car through. No one was hurt and because my engine fell out of the car, it slowed it down drastically before impact. The model of vehicle I was driving was not designed to drop the engine. By hitting the house instead of a tree was also why I survived because the house gave where a tree would not have. I knew I had many angels over that car that day. Too many things worked out that no one was killed or severely injured. I just suffered a minor gash on my hand that only needed a few stitches and some pretty gnarly bruising from the seatbelt. When we went back to see the car later on, the people there were amazed that no one died and all that happened to make it a lot less tragic then it could have been."

I happened to be home alone when I got a call telling me that my daughter was in the hospital. I got bits and pieces from my son-in-law and my mom gave me some details of what had happened. I was living in Maryland at the time, as I mentioned earlier, and she was in Chesapeake, Virginia. I have never been so afraid in my life. My husband was away on military duty and we still had one daughter home. She was in high school at the time, but my place was in Virginia with my elder daughter. I had to talk to my younger daughter and see if she would be all right at home alone. She was seventeen and did not want to go with me, and quite honestly, she couldn't have come with me. She had band practice and she worked part-time. She was able to find a friend whose mother insisted that she come to stay with them. I packed my things and headed to Virginia.

My daughter was released after being in the hospital for a few hours. She needed help in the shower and her husband could not help there, because his knee had just been stitched up. He had had surgery and the stitches had just been removed. The doctor had even told him that he would be okay, as long as he wasn't in any car accident! Well, he was in that accident and the knee opened back up. I decided to help my daughter in the shower. After all, I am her mother and I had bathed and changed her often enough when she was a child. My heart sank to my stomach when I saw her. Her skin was all black and blue from the accident. When I say she was all black and blue, I mean it. I don't think there was any flesh color on her body. I wanted to cry. To this day, I cannot look at the pictures of her car. It was totaled.

〰

I had been at church on a Wednesday night (still in Pasadena, Maryland). My daughters and my elder daughter's future husband were all sitting in our living room, when I came in and greeted everyone. They all looked at me strangely and then my husband called me into the kitchen to talk to me. I wondered what I had done wrong. My husband sat me down and told me, "Your mom is okay, but she has been shot." It took a moment to let the last part of that sentence sink in. No! I thought to myself. There is no way my mom could have been shot. Who would shoot my mother? It turned out to be a complete accident, and was not done out of malice. If the bullet had gone a fraction of an inch away from where it actually did, my mother would not be with us today. It just missed her heart and major arteries and veins.

She was calm in the ambulance, and the attendants were very surprised, telling her that her heart rate and respiration were normal, as was her blood pressure. They asked her how she had managed to keep these signs normal, she said that she had prayed and had placed her life in God's hands. The attendants told her she was truly blessed and that every one of them in that ambulance were also believers.

〰

A few months after we moved to Hawaii the biggest miracle happened. Our youngest had been accepted to Virginia Tech and was attending in the Cadet Corps (the section of the college for men and women who plan to join the military, or want the structure that the military provides). She had finally settled into being a college student, after we had gone through the tears in the beginning, when she wanting to quit and come home. We told her that she should not quit, but finish the first semester, and then, if she still felt she wanted to go elsewhere, we would allow her to. She decided to stay, and during her second semester there, I was sleeping in bed and my husband woke me up. He told me that there had been a shooting at Virginia Tech. I sat straight up but he assured me our daughter was safe. Of course, I did not believe him – I had to hear from her myself. We kept trying to contact her but had no success, as the lines were down. Finally, she was able to get in contact with us, and from what she said to us, she had truly lived through a miracle. She was meant to go to a particular building to study before her class, but something told her to stay in her room, so she did. The shooting happened in the building where she was meant to go. I pray for my daughters regularly, and just before going to sleep I had prayed for God to keep my daughter safe. The time difference between Virginia and Hawaii is about six hours, so I was praying about the time our daughter got up for the day. I truly believe God told her to stay in her room and not go to that building, and He had protected her as I had asked Him to do.

〰

We moved back to Maryland after five years of living in Hawaii. What a bummer, I thought, but we were going where God wanted us to be. About six months after moving to Maryland, our older daughter, her husband and their daughter, moved back to the USA from Germany, to Oklahoma.

They arrived in Oklahoma, found and bought a house, and settled into their new life. Things looked really good for them. A year later, I was at the gym working out and I saw a TV report of a huge tornado. This was a F5 tornado, one of the biggest there is, in Moore, Oklahoma, where my daughter was living. I hurried home and tried to reach her on the phone, but I couldn't do it, because the lines were busy.

I kept my eyes on the TV to see if I could see their house which I had visited, so I knew what I was looking for. The phone rang, and it was my daughter. I fell on my knees and started crying. She told me this big tornado on TV was not the first tornado that week, and they had been having tornadoes all week.

I prayed for God to surround their house with His angels and to cover their house with His blood (like the time of the Israelites during the original Passover) and to fill their house with His Holy Spirit. I tell you that when you pray that kind of prayer, you can expect to see a big miracle.

In this case, every tornado missed them. Even cars at the end of their street flipped over. The only thing that happened to them was that their fence fell down, and everything else stayed as it was. They had to go into the closet because they did not have a storm shelter. The big F5 was only a little more than a mile from their house. My daughter went out later and took pictures of the devastation, and I was shocked to see the damage. Even the theater where my daughter had taken pictures of me and my granddaughter was damaged. God protected my family. All because I prayed and believed. Faith no greater than a mustard seed is all that it takes.

ख

Chapter 14
Miracle in our finances

"Bring ye all the tithes into the storehouse, that there may be meat in mine house, and prove me now herewith, saith the LORD of hosts, if I will not open you the windows of heaven, and pour you out a blessing, that there shall not be room enough to receive it." **Malachi 3:10**

My second husband and I struggled financially for years. I came into our marriage with nothing but two daughters, a large credit card bill and no money. He came with a townhouse on which he owed money, payments on a truck, a couple of credit card bills, child support payment, and nothing left over. We did the best we could. I worked part-time, and he worked four jobs. He would work graveyard shift at the shipyard five nights/mornings a week, worked for a small engine repair shop two days a week, worked for a landscaping company two days a week, and with the Army Reserves for one weekend each month and twenty-eight days during the summer. Still, we were strapped. I would try to figure ways to stretch out the dollars to pay for the food while giving our three daughters a life to remember. We would go camping once a month in the summer because it only cost eight dollars for a tent camp site. We would take the girls to the water park after five because it was half price in the summer, and the beach after five because parking was free then.

The Army Reserves gave him the chance to go full-time, and he took it. Our money almost doubled, but so did the debts. We couldn't sell the townhouse without losing our shirts, so we opted to rent it out. We bought another house at our first duty station and we had to make sure we could afford both places, if for some reason the townhouse went unrented for any length of time. You can only start to imagine the home we bought. We had to fix so many things that went wrong. In the end, we had to replace every pipe in the plumbing because of the leaks. My husband fell through the bathtub one time! That meant we had to repair the subfloors – and of course, we had to buy a new bathtub. We sunk so much money into the place that again, when time came to move, we could not sell the place.

At our next duty station, we bought another house approved by the VA, which meant we did not have to put any money down. We settled in and started to enjoy our new home, but again, the debts got bigger. We had to buy new vehicles because the ones we had were falling apart and costing more than it was worth to keep them going. We had to buy materials on credit to get the home livable. Then there was the money we had to pay to fix things in the townhouse and the other house. We were sinking. Our credit card debt alone was over forty-five thousand dollars. When we came to figure it all out, we were in the hole for over a quarter of a million dollars. I was scared. If something were to happen to my husband, I would have had to file bankruptcy, and that is something that I was taught that you never do, and that you paid off your debts. I started praying.

What I was shown as an answer to my prayer was that we were not going to church anywhere. We had basically turned our backs on God without completely turning our backs on Him. Confused? You see, God tells us not to stop ourselves from assembling together. We are to come together to worship God. We are to be an encouragement to our brothers and sisters in Christ. We had to get back into church.

In the local paper, I saw that a church was starting up, with the first meeting on 1 April. I called the number and talked to the pastor, telling him that we were looking for a home church, and that the name of the church had caught my attention. He and his wife came by and talked with us.

We attended that first Sunday and every Sunday after that. When they started holding Sunday evening services, we attended those as well, and then Wednesday nights. I ended up going to every single service held by this church. After about two months of going, another "aha moment" hit me. Nothing was said out loud in church, just the Holy Spirit speaking to me in my heart. I was told that we needed to start tithing. I told my husband this, and he looked at me as though I had lost my mind. Where were we going to come up with that kind of money to give one tenth of our income? We were living paycheck to paycheck as it was. There was nothing left over to put anywhere. I knew we had to give, so I worked it out. I would write the check for the tithe first thing on payday and then I would write out the other bills. Everything got paid, groceries were bought – and what a surprise! We saw money left over. Enough money that we did not have to borrow money for our gas.

After this had gone on for a few months, I started increasing the check to the church by about five dollars for the mission field. I also increased repayments on one credit card by about five or ten dollars, imagining we would be back to paycheck to paycheck. Another surprise – we actually had even more money left over! My husband did not believe what he was seeing.

We reached a stage where we were able to sell the townhouse. We searched for an agent and then went on a small vacation, and on the way home from the vacation, our agent called us and asked if we could meet him. He told us we had four bids for the house, and they were more than what we were asking for the place by about ten thousand dollars. We closed on the house and took the money to pay off a couple of the smaller credit card bills, and when we'd done that, we cut up the cards and closed them out. I now set my mind to switching the amounts I had been paying on those cards over to the next card, where I owed less.

My husband and I had five- and ten-year financial plans. We were ahead of schedule, and when he got a raise, the amount we gave to the church also increased, as did the amount to missions. We met our ten-year goal in five years. We received orders to move, and we looked for an agent to sell our house where we were living. Again, we got more for the house than we were asking. With this money, not only were we able to move, we could pay off all of our credit cards and both of our new cars.

We did not want to take any chances, so when we arrived at our new duty station, we set out right away to find a church. God has been so faithful and He has proved to us that we cannot give Him more than He can give us. His blessings have been abundant and overflowing. We still own the one house at our first duty station and our middle daughter and her husband are looking to buy that one from us soon. We have another home in our last duty station with seven and a half acres of land. We just bought a new car in February 2014 and now (July 2015), we owe a little over four thousand dollars on this car. We have been able to pay for three weddings, colleges for our daughters and for ourselves, and put a significant amount in our savings account. We are not rich by any means, but we are comfortable right now. We don't hoard our money. We still give our tithes and offerings, and sometimes buy a grocery gift card anonymously and have our pastor give it. We take people out to lunch, which surprises them when we invite them. We give generously the way God wants us to give. We are not foolish with it. We do pray about it first and we do talk it over, but we help where we can. We also give of ourselves for our church family.

My point is not to brag about what we are doing, because I am telling you this to honor God, not for our own glory. My point is that we were told to give by God and we listened. The miracle is that we are no longer living paycheck to paycheck and the glory all goes to God.

Chapter 15
More Time Together

*"Of whom the whole family in heaven and
earth is named,"* **Ephesians 3:15**

I love my family. My parents are a good example of a good and
Godly unit. They raised my sister, brother and myself to do the
best we can in life and to live life for God.

I also love my in-laws. My mother-in-law and father-in-law did a
wonderful job in raising a man to be a good spiritual leader and a
wonderful husband and father.

I want to especially talk about my father-in-law, whom we called
"Pop." What a wonderful man. I have never heard him say anything bad against anyone. In fact, when we were all together for a
family dinner and anyone at the table started to talk badly about
someone else, he would gently put a stop to the conversation and
change the topic to something good.

One day, my husband had to go on a temporary assignment for
the Army. My car would not start and I needed to go somewhere.
I called my dad, but he was not home, and my brother lived too
far away, so I called Pop. I was expecting him to be his usual kind
self and come help me. Instead, I received a lecture on how it was
wrong of me to have my husband work all of the time and how I
should go out and find a job. I had a job, though it was part-time,
but it was a job and it helped us with what we needed. Since my
daughter was suffering from seizures, I was let go from many jobs
because I had to spend a lot of time at the hospital. I was in tears
until my neighbor came over and fixed my car.

I told my husband about this, and said that this was not like his
dad at all. He called his mom to see what was going on, but she
did not know. His dad would complain of a headache, but when

they would go to the doctor, he would talk about how he was going to the restroom so much. So instead of checking his head, they would check his prostate.

A few months later, we discovered that he could not remember the names of restaurants that he would frequent. He was forgetting the names of people, and his driving got really bad. He had several near misses on the road. This worried and scared my mother-in-law. She talked to the doctor, but he was no help.

Pop was getting worse. My mother-in-law went to the doctor once more and demanded to have something done – an MRI starting at the head and ending at the feet. She knew something was very wrong and she wanted to get to the bottom of it. She thought of the idea of an MRI because my daughter had just had one due to a seizure.

An MRI was scheduled and when the technician saw the results, he called the doctor right away, and they were looking at the images when a neurosurgeon walked by. He glanced over, saw the images and said to them, "Get that patient in here now." My father-in-law had a tumor in the frontal lobe of his brain about the size of the palm of a full grown man's hand, and it had to come out.

The family was called. My sister-in-law had to fly in from Michigan and was due to land at the moment the surgery began. My husband said he would go with me, and we would pick her up from the airport. On our way there, he told me that he could see the operating room and a hand reaching over the doctor's shoulder and grabbing hold of the tumor. My reply was that he just has to believe. We talked on the subject of faith and at that moment we saw a white Cadillac, with gold trim framing the license plate with the word BELIEVE (the state had just approved seven letter license plates.) I looked over at my husband and said, "Do you need God to hit you upside your head?" He was in shock.

After picking up my sister-in-law, and telling her the story so far, we made it back to the hospital, and not long after we arrived, the operation was completed. Pop made it through. Miracle number one; the doctor only gave him a forty percent chance of surviving the surgery.

However, the tumor was a large one. The surgeon could remove it, but the tumor had branches that went deep into the brain, and the surgeon was unable to remove these. My father-in-law was given a year, at the most, of good quality life.

Almost a year later Pop was doing fine, but in one month's time, he went to being worse than he was before. The cancer was back – with a vengeance – he didn't have much time left.

While dealing with this news and taking care of Pop, my mother-in-law had a mammogram, and the results was a diagnosis of breast cancer. She refused to have a mastectomy and opted for radiation treatment, which meant both she and Pop were both undergoing radiation treatment. My husband was running back and forth to the hospital with his parents, working at a job where he had been given a pink slip three times, and three times having it pulled back. He was working in the civil service and there was a reduction in forces in place. The Army Reserves offered him a full-time position which he said he definitely wanted, but explained his situation, and asked if the starting date could be pushed back as far as possible. They could push it back a few months, but that is the best they could manage, and he would have to leave to train in June.

The family got together to celebrate Easter and Mother's Day together. June came around and my husband had to leave for Wisconsin, but on the day he left, my father-in-law ended up bedridden, and had to use the hospice at home service. I often went by to visit him and my mother-in-law and sit with him while she went for her check-ups. It was really hard to see a man who had always been very athletic, very intelligent, loving history, just lying in bed, not talking, just a shell of the man he had been.

The morning of the day my husband was to take his final exams and fly home, my phone rang and it was my mother-in-law. She didn't have to say anything. I said the words, "He's gone." He had passed away in his sleep.

My husband called me while he was at the airport and asked me how Pop was doing. I didn't know how to answer him at first. But then I remembered the discussions Pop and I had had about salvation and I knew without a doubt that he had gone home. Before I could say anything, my husband asked me, "He is gone, isn't he?" I told him yes, he had gone. He asked me when and I told him that it happened in the wee hours this morning.

But how is this a miracle, you may ask? We were given another year with a wonderful man. We were given the opportunity to get together as a family, which might not have happened if it hadn't been for this. During that time, we laughed, we cried, we just went through the motions, and we experienced everything. During the viewing, we stood over his coffin and looked down on him. He looked so peaceful, wearing his Air Force uniform.

We got some strange looks from people when we would remember something funny that he used say to mom during the last few weeks, and we would break out laughing. There are five stages of mourning, we got through the first few stages during his illness. What was left was acceptance and relief. The blessing was he never really suffered because he never knew where he was or what year he was in. It was we who suffered, seeing him deteriorate before our eyes.

Never take a second for granted. Tell those whom you love that you love them and go to see them. Nothing is worth keeping you away from your parents or your children. Spend time together every chance you can get. And by the way, my mother-in-law has been cancer-free since that time.

Part II
Testimony of Miracles as Experienced By Others

This section recounts miracles that have been witnessed or experienced by others. Some are in-depth accounts, while others are summaries. To God be the glory and honor in these testimonies of miracles.

My comments on how I have come to know the person testifying are in italics, and I will give views from my perspective about the miracle.

I do hope you enjoy these.

๑๛

Chapter 16
A Miracle Baby for Us

"Before I formed you in the womb, I knew you. Before you were born, I set you apart for my holy purpose. I appointed you to be a prophet to the nations." **Jeremiah 1:5**

This family was told to terminate a pregnancy because of some complications seen by the doctors. Because of their beliefs, they could not do this.

〰

M y daughter is a miracle. I was pregnant with our daughter the day before Mother's Day and two days before my husband left for a nine-month deployment. I was staying at our home in Washington State with our three-year-old son. The day I dropped off my husband for deployment I had some cramping and went to the ER where they told me it was one of four things. One, it was too early; two, it was ectopic; three, I was going to miscarry, or; four, I was miscarrying. In the next four weeks I went every week to the doctor to have blood drawn to check my hormone levels and have an ultrasound scan.

As the weeks went by I saw my child grow, and I was relieved. One day while on the phone with a friend I started bleeding. I was seventeen weeks pregnant and had to go to the ER since it was too early to head to labor and delivery. I sat and waited fearing for the worst. After two hours I was seen and told that I had experienced a placental abruption. Part of the placenta had come off of the uterus wall. I was put on bed rest and told to follow up with my doctor in a few days. The placenta healed enough for me to resume regular activity

At the twenty-week anatomy scan I reclined in joyful

anticipation with a friend to share the moment. I couldn't wait to see what we had coming our way and to share the news with my husband when he called that night. I had. After the tech told me it was a girl I could not stop smiling. My husband had said he thought it was a girl and I knew he would be beyond excited. Then the tech became quiet but I didn't think anything at the time. I just sat there staring at the picture of the baby.

I returned to the waiting room eagerly waiting for the nurse to tell me that I could leave and follow up with my regular doctor's appointment. I waited and waited, and then started complaining to my friend that they needed to hurry up, as I needed to fetch my son from the sitter.

Almost thirty minutes passed before a colonel[1] came to the door asking me to step into another room with him. I panicked and could hardly breathe. He told me my daughter was small – in the 10th percentile and that she had a large hole in her heart and that I needed to have an amniocentesis done to test whether or not it was genetic. I declined the test because I did not want to add any more stress to my little girl.

Every two weeks I had to have an ultrasound scan to check her heart and growth. At thirty-seven weeks they told me that the hole was still present, and that she would be evaluated by a cardiologist after she was born. After three false labors and being a week overdue I was beyond ready to give birth.

On January 15th I started contractions – thankfully, since they had scheduled me for an induction on the 16th. After I had been monitored for about an hour, they told me to take a walk and come back.

My friend, who was supposed to take my three-year-old son, did not answer her phone and therefore he was with us. We broke the rules and ran to get him dinner. After we got him something to eat, I told my husband to stop at the base shoppette[2] because I

1 This was a military hospital
2 This is what the military calls its convenience stores.

had to use the restroom, but I barely made it out.

Since it was after nine and I told my husband there was no way I was going to make it to the emergency room. I was in the restroom AGAIN because I had to go, except this time I could feel my daughter's head and I was bleeding again. My husband ran through the halls yelling for help. A couple passing by went to the labor and delivery department to tell them that a woman (me!) was having a baby in the restroom and twelve doctors and nurses squeezed into the tiny two-stall restroom. Twenty minutes after reentering the hospital, I gave birth to my daughter who was rushed to a waiting incubator in the hall, with all the pediatric nurses and doctors in attendance. They could still hear her heart murmur (the hole) and said she would be evaluated as soon as they could get her into the examining room.

Our miracle occurred three weeks later when they did all the tests and could see no evidence of any heart condition. God had healed our precious girl whom they had advised us to terminate.

She turned six on the 15th and we joke that we prayed for her life so hard she has extra!"

⚜

I met this lady on social media. We are in the same group and she sent me this miracle when I asked if anyone wanted to share their miracles.

ᦖ

Chapter 17
Angel, Baby and Husband

"Let your conversation be without covetousness; and be content with such things as ye have: for he hath said, I will never leave thee, nor forsake thee." **Hebrews 13:5**

I had graduated from high school and moved back south into our old house. I had one roommate left from the three that lived there, and she and her boyfriend and I were the only ones in the house. My boyfriend had to be at the Civic Center to baby-sit the Christmas Trees to make sure nobody would steal them. We were experimenting with the ouija board. I know, you had always warned me about them and would not allow them in your home. I was curious. Afterwards, I felt very uncomfortable, as if something was following me and laughing at me. I went to my room and started praying asking for forgiveness and asking God to fill my room with the Holy Spirit. I called my boyfriend and told him how uncomfortable I was and asked if I could be with him. He said it would be okay, so I left and sat with him watching the trees. My roommate and her boyfriend did not know that I had left. Her boyfriend had to go to the bathroom, which was located across from my bedroom. I had the door to my room closed. When he walked by my room and looked at the door of my bedroom, he saw a very bright light shining around the edges of my door and under my door. He thought I was messing with something. He opened the door to look in, but there was nothing. It made him a little nervous.

Later again. My boyfriend and I had broken up. I had just had his baby and was going through postpartum depression. I was really down and depressed. It was so bad that a couple of times I thought about suicide. I was really going through a rough time being a single mom and everything. I knew I was in love with the daddy of my baby and knew I wanted to be back with him but didn't want to seem needy. One night, while I was on the couch, I was crying out to God. I don't know my purpose or what you want from me. Life is not what I envisioned for myself. What do you want from me? What do I do about my baby's daddy? I heard a voice. Not audibly but from within. He was speaking to my heart not my ears, I heard "Be patient." I said to Him, "What do you mean? I don't understand." I heard Him again saying, "Be patient" so I said, "Okay, I leave it in your hands." I really feel deep down in my heart that God spoke to me and not my guardian angel.

A couple of months later, my baby's daddy and I went to the Child Support Agency to have child support go through the courts. We rode together in his truck. When we got there, I could not get out. I mean that I could not physically move. We went to the beach instead and talked. He had been trying to get back with me, but I didn't know what to do. I wasn't sure. He was saying how he would be faithful and everything. I had said that I would not get back together unless we got married. He said he was even ready to get married. I was quiet and said a quiet prayer to God, that if this was meant to be and he was the one for me, God would show me a sign. Two shooting stars crossed over each other and I took this as confirmation. I said, "Yes," and we were married four days later.

❦

I remember the day my daughter called and told me she was pregnant. There she was, a young adult, unmarried and scared. I had to tell her that she was not the first to have a baby outside marriage and she will not be the last. She was so upset, but I reassured her that we and she will get through this.

When she was twelve, she met a boy, who later became the father of her baby. He lived across the street and would really annoy her. Every day, on the school bus, he would chant to her that he loved her and that he was going to marry her, even though he was only ten at this time. She would come home so upset, and beg me to tell him to stop. I told her that the day they got married, I was going to laugh. I was living in Hawaii and she was still in North Carolina. She called me and told me that they had got married at the courthouse and all I could do was laugh. We did have a marriage ceremony a few months later, in 2007, because he told me that he had ruined things for her and he felt she deserved one. It was a wonderful celebration. Their daughter walked her daddy down the aisle. My daughter had her dad and her stepdad walk side by side in front of her like her guards and escort, and it was beautiful. This was in 2007 and just like all marriages, they have had their ups and downs. They now have two children together, their daughter and their son. To me this is another miracle.

ও৫

Chapter 18
By His Stripes

"Heal me, O LORD, and I shall be healed; save me, and I shall be saved: for thou art my praise." **Jeremiah 17:14**

"You want me to tell you a miracle? Right away, I can tell you, it would be my seizure disorder. After years and years of trying medication after medication and test after test with no real answers, and to still have seizures; I just fell to my knees and with my whole heart, prayed for answers and a cure. Next thing I knew, my neurologist sent me off to do a weekly test. I had no seizure disorder. They diagnosed me with pseudo seizures from severe anxiety and panic disorder. With this new information, they started focusing more on my anxiety and panic disorder, and I have now been seizure free for almost eight years. Yeah, I still have some issues, but I'll take the panic and anxiety over seizures any day."

〰

I know how it was for me to have my daughter have these seizures. I would pray many times over her. I would take her to the altar at church. Many nights were spent in the hospital while I waited for test after test that they were doing with her. This was a very trying time for me and I can see God's hands on my own life during this time. He kept me calm, cool and collected and showed me again that He is always with me and most importantly, He is always in control.

ᏜᏜ

Chapter 19
A Child and a Healing

"And God remembered Rachel, and God hearkened to her, and opened her womb" **Genesis 30:22**

The following paragraph is from my aunt. She sent me this response after I asked if she could share a miracle that she has personally experienced.

〰

It is hard to choose just one. You know that my son being here is a miracle. I was supposedly unable to produce a viable egg. One more unusual thing is when I was diagnosed with a blood clot after breaking my foot when trying to sneakily give my parents a microwave oven, and setting it up while they were at dinner. When I next saw my PCP[1] and said I thought I might have a blood clot in my leg, she sent me over to the hospital for testing. Sure enough, I did have a blood clot in my leg, so I was admitted. That night, my PCP could not shake a feeling that she needed to look further, and she contacted the hospital, insisting they do further testing. The results of that test showed a pulmonary embolism (PE) which could have killed me at any moment.

The hospital physicians were shocked, and my PCP was so moved by this intervention from God that she left her home to come and tell me personally about the diagnosis. Since PEs are usually extremely painful, they did not suspect it. When they asked me if I had been in pain, my response had only been that I hurt under my left arm and connected chest area from a pulled muscle after using the crutches for my broken foot. These corresponded to the location of the PE in my lung, but they never

---

1 Primary Care Physician, an abbreviation used in the military

suspected a PE because I was not complaining about pain. Thank God for using my PCP for her willingness to listen to and follow his direction.

〰️

God has a way of bringing people back into your life. I met my aunt for the first time in Biloxi, Mississippi when she was only twelve, and I was six. Of course, this was before she married my uncle and became my aunt. We would wait at the bus stop together sometimes when she was babysitting at the trailer park across the street from the house I lived in at that time.

I remember how much she glowed and how happy she was the whole time she was pregnant with my cousin. When he was born, he was such a beautiful baby boy. I believe, after knowing her briefly as a child and after her marriage to my uncle ended, that she was given my cousin so that we would always be tied together.

I am also thankful for God laying it on her doctor's heart to have a test done and finding the pulmonary embolism. Because of this, she is still with us today. She will always be my aunt, but more importantly, she will be my sister for eternity.

〰️

Chapter 20
Ask in Faith

"But let him ask in faith, nothing wavering. For he that wavereth is like a wave of the sea driven with the wind and tossed." JAMES 1:6

At this time my daughter had just turned two and my son was five.

I came home from work, and I was straightening up a little and getting ready to cook supper. My son was outside playing and my daughter was in the house. My husband, Richard, had gone to the doctor that day for his eyes, and wanted me to help put some eye drops in. My son came back inside and when he went out again, my daughter managed to sneak outside with him, but when I looked up she was on the porch, so I looked down to put the drops in my husband's eyes. He had blinked maybe 8-10 times when my son, Dean, came running in the house and said, "Sissy hurt, Sissy in water, I pull her out." (MIRACLE 1. Dean has autism and at that time there was a huge communication barrier.)

Panic set in. We jumped up and I screamed, "My daughter's on the ground and she's not moving!" I don't know how we managed to get out of the door. It seemed as though our feet never hit the ground and we flew about 15-20 feet to my little girl lying beside the pool. From what we could tell, she must have slipped and fallen into the foot bucket beside the pool, with about four inches of water in it. She must have lost her breath or got knocked out or something.

She was lying on her back with foam and blood coming from her mouth and nose. She wasn't breathing or even attempting to breathe. At that moment I felt my heart stop, and vomit rising in my throat. Here Richard's instincts took over. He flipped her over and stimulated her back, which thankfully caused her to throw up. (MIRACLE 2) He did this several times, and by this time 911 had been called and my in-laws were running over. My brother-in-law told us that our call was the third one for Otway (the small town in North Carolina where we were living) and they only have two ambulances... (More panic) Richard told him to get on the phone and tell them we needed a medic now. He was saying something about ASR and drowning...by that time my head was spinning in several directions and all I could get out was "Please don't take my baby!!!" I was so thankful to my sister-in-law (8 months pregnant!) and her daughter for staying with me, holding me up, and helping me remember to breathe. (MIRACLE 3)

The ambulance got there just as a paramedic arrived, but they didn't even make it into the driveway. My husband ran to the ambulance with my daughter, and instructed his mom to call my mother and take me to the hospital, which she did, in about ten minutes. I called for a police escort to the hospital, but to this day still haven't seen one! My aunt called me at about this time and told me she saw my daughter and she was screaming. (MIRACLE 4)

I thank God for this miracle every day. They let me go straight back and there was my little girl lying there on oxygen, so weak, with all the blood vessels in her eyelids and around broken. I crawled into the bed and held her. The doctor came in and told us they were sending her to Pitt Memorial Hospital[1], and although they had requested an ambulance, Pitt sent a helicopter, which I was glad for, since it was faster.)(MIRACLE 5)

We went back home and got some clothes, and the medic from the helicopter called us and told us our daughter was doing great. Her O2 stats were back up to 99 and 100, without oxygen. (MIRACLE 6)

We arrived at Pitt about 2½ hours later (seemed like much longer). They had already assessed her, so they brought a bed

1 Now known as Vidant Medical Center

instead of a crib for her to sleep in, so I could lie with her . The next morning the doctors came in and said we could go home, since all the fluid was gone and she had been off oxygen all night long. (MIRACLE 7)

So, we came home, and called the doctor who was treating Dean's autism to see if he (my son) needed anything, since he was the one who saw the whole thing and called us. She said it sounded as though he was doing fine, and asked us if we wanted to put my daughter in a hyperbaric chamber, where oxygen is supplied at a higher pressure than usual, because sometimes after a drowning incident days later blood levels would be off and the chamber would prevent that. She did this for us absolutely free (MIRACLE 8).

Wednesday and Thursday we spent in Wilmington with the hyperbaric chamber, and it helped her a lot. I am extremely claustrophobic, so Richard stayed in the chamber with her, and the second time she was in there, she even went to sleep.

We are so amazingly grateful to have a second chance with my daughter, after coming so close to losing her. I never ever want to have that feeling again, and I would never wish it on my worst enemy

A very positive thing came out of it all; I was having doubts about faith and things like that since my father passed away in 2006. All I can say is that my daughter is alive by the grace of God, and all those doubts are completely gone. I know I saw His work that day so many times, and am so truly grateful that He had a hand in helping Richard stay so completely calm and do what needed to be done to save his daughter.

He also had a hand in letting Dean communicate with us and that he knew to come and get us, because after that happened he reverted, and was unable to communicate with us for a while.

My daughter bounced back in no time. She is now nine years old, swims like a fish and is not afraid of the water. My son never had any setbacks with his autism, or dealing with all the traumatic things he saw that day.

I saw God's work at first hand, and had so many miracles happen to me that day. You will never convince me that He wasn't the one who made it all possible."

〰️

This young lady is my son-in-law's cousin, and I remember hearing him speak of this when I visited them.

When I asked my family and friends if they would like to share a miracle they have experienced or witnessed, she did not hesitate. She wanted to share her story. I cannot imagine believing your baby is gone. What a miracle this truly is. The little girl is fine and so full of life. Her son is a beautiful soul and knowing him and hearing of what he did to help save his sister is a miracle in itself.

She gave me two verses for this miracle and I can think of a few more. I started with one of the verses and will end this one with the second verse. God does care about all of our needs and if we truly come to Him in faith, even if it is a small amount of faith, He will hear us.

〰️

That your faith should not stand in the wisdom of men, but in the power of God. **1 Corinthians 2:5**

Chapter 21
Adoption of Children

"Having predestinated us unto the adoption of children by Jesus Christ to himself, according to the good pleasure of his will," **Ephesians 1:5**

It all started when I was thirteen years old. I was saved at the same time as my mom. My father was not a Christian and he would beat my siblings and myself. My mom wanted something for us, so she took us to church. After one service, my mom and I went forward and accepted Christ as our Savior. We were also baptized together, and I will never forget that day. The next miracle came when I married my husband on August 22, 1992, so we will be celebrating twenty-three years of marriage. Four years into our marriage, we decided to try and have a baby, but we were unable to conceive. It turned out to be because of I have only one ovary, and one tube is blocked while the other is damaged. We tried in-vitro fertilization (IVF) but that did not work.

In 2002, my husband, being in the Army, had to go to Korea for a year. He called me up and said, 'let us adopt international.' We started the adoption process when he returned from Korea, and though it was a long road and a lot of paperwork, it was God's will. We adopted a wonderful little girl, from Korea, who was only seventeen months old when she arrived with us. She is now nine, and during Vacation Bible School at our church, she accepted Christ as her Savior, and is now waiting to be baptized. It was my heart's desire to be a mother, and to have this opportunity through adoption is a miracle.

I have two verses for this miracle. The first one is at the top of the page, Ephesians 1:5. The second one is below.

"For God so loved the world, that he gave his only begotten Son, that whosoever believeth in him should not perish, but have everlasting life." **John 3:16**

W

This wonderful woman is a member of my church. I have enjoyed spending time with her and even assisted in teaching the class in Vacation Bible School that her daughter attended. Getting to know this young lady was such a pleasure. She is so intelligent and beautiful. I was there the day she was saved. Her mother was sitting in the sanctuary, at the end of the day, and we had this young lady, along with the other four that accepted Christ, stand on the stage. I was watching her mother while the Pastor explained what had happened that day to these beautiful children. This wonderful woman burst into happy tears when she found out that her daughter had accepted Christ. Seeing her mother cry, this beautiful child also started crying. You have never seen such love as the one that exists between this woman and her daughter. It is so obvious when you see them together. The only love that tops this is in the above verse that she gave. Such a beautiful testimony of a miracle.

Chapter 22
Tiny Miracles, Big Miracles, More Miracles

*"O Lord, my strength, and my fortress, and my refuge
in the day of affliction..." Jeremiah 16:19a*

Sigh. Miracles.

I see them every day, but they are tiny ones, hardly considered as such by most people. A newborn's first breath is a terrific example.

"As for the bigger ones, well, it's more like answered prayer, so don't know if they'd qualify as true miracles:

"Praying for years that my husband would quit smoking—he'd smoked since his teens and was a two plus pack a day smoker (he did quit, but God did it in a rather dramatic way—he had a heart attack and wasn't allowed to smoke while in the hospital, never picked it up again.

An aneurysm took him to the hospital via ambulance (didn't know till I showed up—I took my time. Then, I was told he had a 50/50 chance of survival. I immediately contacted our church's prayer chain then I began praying. He made it (praise God).

With another heart attack, his heart stopped in the ambulance and they had to do CPR to bring him back (again, I didn't know this until I arrived at the hospital). More prayers. He lived. God is good!

With each episode, I had such peace – no worry at all.

Even when he was diagnosed with cancer ... and only lived three very long weeks from diagnosis to passing. God has been there for me throughout my life. I consider myself blessed. So blessed!

One final miracle: a helicopter filled with tourists (including me) eager to see Mount St. Helens, "falling" (engine problems) 1500 feet, we landed safely enough for all passengers to live. We didn't all walk away, but injuries were light—except for one person: a seven-month pregnant woman sitting to my right at the rear of the helicopter. She and the baby were fine.

I have found that there are two Bible passages that seem to weave into my life, helping me through each day:

"He will not grow tired or weary, and his understanding no one can fathom.He gives strength to the weary and increases the power of the weak. Even youths grow tired and weary,and young men stumble and fall; but those who hope in the LORD will renew their strength They will soar on wings like eagles; they will run and not grow weary, they will walk and not be faint." **Isaiah 40:28b-31**

"Lord, you are my strength and fortress, my refuge in the day of trouble!" **Jeremiah 16:19a**

And He is just that! Every single day.

This is a wonderful woman I met on social media and in a writer's group that I am a member of. She is also an author and was just signed up by my publisher. I am honored that she sent me these miracles that she has experienced and witnessed.

Chapter 23
Ask and You will Receive

"And all things, whatsoever ye shall ask in prayer, believing, ye shall receive." **Matthew 21:22**

When my children were little, I needed to do the wash, especially their clothes and the diapers. I had one of those wringer washers, which was located outside on my porch. It was getting ready to rain. I really needed to get that wash done. I went to the front door, looked up at the dark clouds and prayed this prayer. 'Lord, my babies need clean clothes and clean diapers.' While I was praying, I looked up and watched as the clouds parted like the Red Sea and the sun was revealed. God is awesome. I washed clothes all day. Got them all done."

〰

This is from my own mother. I have seen one prayer after another of hers get answered. I am not saying she is perfect and I am sure she has had some prayers unanswered, or answered with "no", but I have seen so many positive answers, as I have written earlier.

I know that my mom is no more special to God than the next believer. God loves us all equally. I believe answers to prayers are connected to belief and faith. As that verse says "whatsoever" you ask for will be given, but there is something to understand. God will not give us millions of dollars because we ask believing. It does not work that way. God is not a bank. He will give us what we need.

☙❧

Chapter 24
Amazing Healing

"Who his own self bare our sins in his own body on the tree,
that we, being dead to sins, should live unto righteousness:
by whose stripes ye were healed. **1 Peter 2:24**

I am a Christian who has fallen many times, but God still continues to work miracles in my life. No amount of luck, fate, or coincidence could describe the things God has done in my life.

When I was twenty-one years old, I began living my dream life. I was a flight attendant for a major airline. I instantly fell in love with this job. However, at the same time, I began noticing that I was not acting or reacting like everyone else in certain circumstances. Normal disappointments were sending me into a blind rage in which I became irrational. I would say the vilest of things to the people I most loved. I could never stay calm and normal for long, unless I was at work. I became very promiscuous, yet couldn't feel any emotions towards my actions. I would wallow in grief after having been intimate with yet another guy I barely knew. I had no filter for my emotions and would often spiral out of control at the slightest provocation, unless I was at work.

After a few years, I tried to speak with my parents about this. Because my dad had dealt with this erratic behavior from my birth mother, he did not want to acknowledge anything was wrong. And my mother, (actually my step-mother) who raised me, was such a strict Christian and her only solution for me was to read my Bible more. I would try to be 'normal.' Oh how I tried, but I failed miserably, which only made me feel worse and go haywire. That is how I felt, like I was always going haywire. I hated being so odd, so misunderstood, it felt like no matter how badly I wanted to be a better Christian, I just couldn't be that. It finally took my dad to realize I was really going through it and my birth mom telling me her story, for me to have the courage to seek counseling.

So with the term 'bipolar' bouncing in my head, I began seeing a psychologist. He agreed with the diagnosis. It was great being able to tell him how I really felt. A few specific issues surfaced, anger at my dad, my obsessive sexual promiscuity and my co-dependence on my best friend. Therapy was good for me, but it didn't really change my situations.

During this time, my episodes began to increase in intensity. I was embarrassing my family. I was always in 'crisis,' I was becoming dangerously promiscuous at an alarming rate, with only feelings of ambivalence afterwards. During these few years, I'd been committed two different times for suicide attempts and suicide ideation. Again, I tried to explain to my family what was happening, but by then, too much damage had been done and they didn't want to hear about it or deal with it. I felt so alone. My best friend never left my side, even though he had experienced the brunt end of my episodes. He and his family were there for me and that was such a blessing.

During the roughest times, I'd go back to church and try to get myself together. It was only a temporary thing, because once I had some semblance of stability, I'd forget all about going and trying. I remember clearly when I had my next breakthrough.

I remember being in the beauty shop and was telling my hair stylist about the many guys that I've been with and only in a two week span. It was then that I realized that what I was doing wasn't quite normal, because, you see, I was feeling ambivalent about the whole thing, about the guys I slept with, I never really felt anything afterwards. I didn't feel any guilt, any shame, I just didn't feel anything. It was that day, at the beauty shop, that I realized the behavior I was displaying in the feelings I was having, weren't normal. I said a quick prayer and asked the Lord for help.

Clearly, therapy alone wasn't working, I ended up reaching out to a friend that lives all the way across the country. I told him that I had some anxiety about locating a psychiatrist. I felt like I needed extra help. That friend was able to do a little research and he got me the name of a good psychiatrist. I went to that psychiatrist, but before I went to the appointment, I had people praying for me and praying also that he would be able to diagnose the problem and would be able to treat me with the right medication or therapy. I wanted something that would work for me without me having to go through months of bad side effects.

That is exactly what happened. I went to the psychiatrist and he prescribed me two different medications to take. I can honestly say almost immediately things began to get better. When I say things got better, I mean it was as if I calmed down a bit. I was prescribed a medium dose of Prozac to eliminate my obsessive compulsion for sex. I was officially diagnosed with a sexual obsessive compulsive disorder.

After taking Prozac for the first time, it was very odd for me to not have a sex drive. I felt like I didn't know who I was. I didn't know myself at all and it was a bit hard to discover who I was without being sexual. It took me a couple of weeks to balance out my medication and my sexuality. The doctor also put me on a mood stabilizer which curbed a lot of the episodes that I was having. There was an obvious difference. It helped me calm down a bit and it was such a blessing to get the help I needed. Also, it was a blessing to have my dad to come around and actually listen to me and acknowledge that I was having a problem similar to that of my birth mother. It was also a help to me having him acknowledge this. The medication was really helping me. Things weren't perfect, but they were a little better than they were many times before.

I had to take the medication every day, there would be times where I would stop taking it. I would get lazy, or I would feel as though I was well enough to get off the meds. I would go without for two weeks and then I would start having really bad meltdowns. These were really bad episodes and breakdowns. I would take out terrible actions on my best friend and my family. Then I would have to start the healing process all over again, because they were all embarrassed again. But my best friend stuck by me. He and his family stuck by me even though I put them through so much drama as a result of my life. They were still with me.

The biggest turning point of my life came when I found out my best friend had a daughter and he had never told me about her before. When I found that out, it was probably the lowest point of my life. I literally lost it, I was terrible wreck. I was so depressed, I was doing really crazy things. Because I was not handling my grief and my anger appropriately, I ended up being committed to the hospital. This got me to see that what I needed was a real change of heart. I needed to fall on my knees and be honest with myself and be honest with the Lord.

During this time, the Lord used one of my 'spiritual' moms to teach me about falling on my face before God and even if I have to cry it out, or, to be honest, "smarted it out", and that God was where my sole source of strength and hope and peace was going to come from. In that worst moment of my life, it was like God was directly speaking to me, at the time when I wanted to die, and I literally did want to die when I came out of the hospital after being there for a week.

I immediately went to church and began to truly see how I needed God all of the time, not just when I was in crisis mode. I began to see a difference. I began to hear the Lord and He was able to fill me with that peace that passes understanding. Things did change.

I began to stay in God's word, I began to continue going to church, even when the crisis had passed, I stayed with it. I made it a daily part of my life, just like I had to take medicine every day, I made being close to the Lord a priority in my life, not just someone to go to during the rough time. That was the biggest change for me.

There are still times that I would fail, there were still times that I would stop taking the medication and have to suffer the consequences and do damage control. I have lost some friends and I have alienated some more of my family, but now I have a strong foundation in the Lord. I knew that no matter how bad things got, I was always reminded to fall on my knees before the Lord. There were a lot of times when I didn't want to, and I wanted to nurse my grief and my anger; but eventually, I knew what I needed to do. I needed to call out to the Lord and I did. You know, the enemy doesn't like to see us get on our feet and turn to the Lord. He will always try to separate us from the love of God.

Three years ago, I was going through some problems, and in a weak moment, I ended up in a relationship that was not godly. I was having an affair with one of my co-workers and for a year and a half, I lived that sort of life and I knew I was wrong. I talked to the Lord about it just about every day, but I didn't have the strength to end that relationship. I felt as if I was stuck. I was getting some of my emotional needs met while damaging my basic and spiritual needs, but you know, when we are caught up in something, it is hard to get out of it. I just kept praying for the Lord to give me the strength to make the right decision.

It seemed that when I finally found the strength to leave, all hell broke loose and I was let go from my job with the airlines. I was devastated, crushed, and angry, but I knew from past experiences that, above all else, I needed to trust in God. The relationship ended because I no longer had that job.

Now I had no job, no insurance and I needed my medication, because without it I would end up in crisis mode. I was afraid I would have a terrible episode and do some pretty destructive things to myself. I'd lost my job, but I knew I had to trust in God and so this is what I did, which was against my flesh, I went to church, I studied my Bible, I prayed, I talked with God about my feelings. I didn't notice immediately, but after some months something dawned on me.

I'd been off my medication ever since I lost my job and I was perfectly fine. I had no episodes, no crisis. It was as if I had been healed and I hadn't even realized it. All those months with no medication and I was fine. I realized that God is so faithful because without insurance, I couldn't afford those medications and I was on a pretty hefty dosage of both. I didn't have any relapses, I didn't become sexually promiscuous again. It was as if I was still on the medication, but I wasn't because I didn't have any left.

That is my miracle that God performed for me. After struggling since the age of nineteen with mental issues and being on heavy medication which could not be stopped without consequences for at least five years, I was fine. I had literally gone months and months without the medication after I lost my job and my affair, and I was perfectly fine.

God kept me in perfect peace, and that passage in Paul's second letter to Timothy, saying, "God has not given us a spirit of fear, but of power and love and a sound mind" is so true. God literally worked a miracle in my life and kept me free of medication. It is three years since all that happened to me, and I am still not on any medication, I have not been to the hospital, I have not been suicidal.

Sure there have been times in my life that I have been upset and depressed, but never to the point of suicide. Even when I had to do jobs that I hated, He was with me the whole time, teaching me, being by my side, letting me know how faithful He is, that He never forgets me, that He will never leave me alone, that He is always working things out for my good and now I am back at even a better job and airline than I was before.

There are four verses of Scripture that have helped me most. God's word is full of His promises; sometimes you need more than one. My favorite is that passage where Paul asks God three times to remove the thorn from his flesh. God answers him.

> *"And he said unto me, My grace is sufficient for thee: for my strength is made perfect in weakness. Most gladly therefore will I rather glory in my infirmities, that the power of Christ may rest upon me"* **2 Corinthians 12:9**

My second is the one I quoted above:

> *"For God hath not given us the spirit of fear; but of power, and of love, and of a sound mind."* **2 Timothy 1:7**

My third is the one where Paul says he can do all things through Jesus Christ who strengthens him.

> *"I can do all things through Christ which strengtheneth me."* **Philippians 4:13**

And my fourth verse is written by Peter, when he writes that by His stripes we are healed.

> *"Who his own self bare our sins in his own body on the tree, that we, being dead to sins, should live unto righteousness: by whose stripes ye were healed."* **1 Peter 2:24**

※

This young lady is like a daughter to me. I have been through so much with her. There were times when she was wanting to give up, that she would call me and I would talk to her and encourage her. I would remind her to go take these worries and cares to God, and tell her to fall on her knees. When she told me that she was really angry with God, I would tell her to go tell Him about that. He is the type of friend who wants to know this. Of course, I know He already knows, but He wants us to go to Him and tell Him how we feel.

I would also get calls from my friend about her triumphs. I have seen such a spiritual growth in this young lady, whom I love, and of whom I am very proud.

ও৲৩

Chapter 26
Life and Death

"In the way of righteousness is life: and in the pathway thereof there is no death." **Proverbs 12:28**

This miracle is about my grandma. We were always very close. Once, we talked about dying and I told her that if there is a beautiful place, to please send me a sign. My grandma suffered a stroke and while I was sitting with her, she was talking to people who have already passed. She would say to them, 'I will be there soon.' She then asked me 'did I make it into the obituaries?' I told her yes. My grandma passed a week later. I went to visit her grave after she was buried, on a rainy day. I was crying and telling her how much I missed her. All of a sudden, the sun came through the trees. It was so bright on my face. I knew, at that moment, that there was another side and she showed me. I felt her presence there.

This miracle is about when I was born. I was born prematurely, and the doctor told my parents that I had only twenty-four hours to live and put me into an incubator. My mom went down to the hospital chapel and prayed and prayed. I was in the incubator for two weeks. My mom wanted to name me either Hope or Faith and my dad said Hope. Because of their prayers and their faith, I survived. I feel so blessed. I know I have a purpose here and I believe in our Lord Jesus Christ and God. I know He has always watched over me and my family. Thank you, Lord. That is my story.

❖

I met this wonderful lady through social media. We played a game together, and ended up in a few groups together. She is a lady with a heart of gold, and I asked her if she had a miracle to share for this book, and she sent the above to me as quickly as she could. I am so thankful to our Father that He answered her mother's prayer. And yes, I agree that she does have a purpose here.

Too Many Miracles

---

*"My sheep hear my voice, and I know them,
and they follow me:" John 10:27*

There were a couple of others from whom I had hoped to
have received testimonies of miracles in their lives, but circumstances have prevented them.

🐾

One is from a young man in our church who told me his testimony the first day I went there. He told me of a time that
he was deeply into Satanic worship, and was preparing to be a
priest in that belief. He told me of a car accident that put him in
a coma for several months, and then the pastor told me how the
doctors were preparing his family for his imminent death. Then
the young man told me of the day he woke up and of how this
led him to the Lord. I can tell you from my meetings with this
young man, he is definitely on fire for the Lord. I was hoping to
get his testimony from him, but he has been attending his fian-
cée's church recently, and I have not been able to speak with him.

🐾

Another is from a man in my Sunday School class, now fighting cancer for the fourth time in his life, and each time he
has been at the fourth stage. This stage usually carries the death
sentence – most people do not survive this stage. He would go
to our pastor and the leaders in our church and ask for anointing
and prayer which would be done, and he would end up cancer
free. Right now, he is dealing with bleeding around the brain. I
am sure that writing his testimony is the last thing on his mind.

❦

Miracles are all around us. Just take a look at a humming-bird. It is so small and its wings move so fast that it actually buzzes like an insect. Look at a bumblebee, in their design, I was told they should never have the capability to fly.

Look at plants. Small seeds can grow to be vegetables, bushes, or even huge trees.

Look at babies really closely. Watch how much they learn in a year alone. Look how they are put together. Look at their sonograms while they are in the womb.

Look at animals in general. They don't worry about anything, not about where they will sleep for the night (or day) or where they will get their food. They know it is provided for them.

The rain that falls, the sun that shines, even our planets stay on the same path without going into the sun.

❦

I have experienced so many miracles in my 54 years of life. And from what was sent to me, I can see others experience them as well. Some of the miracles that are not explained by doctors or science. Some so outrageous, that if they weren't experienced firsthand, wouldn't be believed. I know I will experience more miracles. I am excited to see what these will be.

No, there are too many miracles that happens for anyone to convince me that God does not exist. I know He exists. I know He loves me. I also know He loves you too. How? Because the Bible tells me so. The Bible is the only book that has lasted from generation to generation and has not changed. Science books have changed, history books have changed, but the Bible remains the same.

It is God's love letter to us. God is the same today as He was yesterday and as He will be tomorrow. He loves you. How much? He spread His arms on that cross and died for you and me. He defeated death and rose up again from the grave.

All we have to do is accept His free gift of eternal life. It is a gift, one that is never taken back. Acknowledge Him, believe that He was born to a virgin, that He gave His life on that cross for you, that He rose up from the grave and that He is sitting at the right hand side of the Father.

Pray to Him. Ask Him to forgive you of your sins. Accept Him as your Savior. Do so before it is too late. He is coming back again. He is going to call all that believe on Him and have given Him their lives and accepted Him to be with Him for eternity

We are human and we make mistakes. The difference being a Christian and not being a Christian is that we are forgiven. We strive to live more like Christ, but we will not be perfected until the day we go home to heaven. Until that time, I will sing praises to Him and worship Him. I will pray and strive to live for Him. I will also enjoy the miracles that He causes to happen on a daily basis.

May God be glorified in this book. I do hope you have enjoyed reading this, and I pray that you will see the miracles around you a little more clearly.

www.ingramcontent.com/pod-product-compliance
Lightning Source LLC
Chambersburg PA
CBHW070204060426
42445CB00032B/1181